PRACTIC
SOCIAL W

Series Editor: Jo Campling

[BASW]

Editorial Advisory Board:
Terry Bamford, Malcolm Payne, Patrick Phelan,
Peter Riches, Daphne Statham, Jane Tunstill,
Sue Walrond-Skinner, and Margaret Yelloly

Social work is at an important stage in its development. All professions must be responsive to changing social and economic conditions if they are to meet the needs of those they serve. This series focuses on sound practice and the specific contribution which social workers can make to the well-being of our society in the 1990s.

The British Association of Social Workers has always been conscious of its role in setting guidelines for practice and in seeking to raise professional standards. The conception of the Practical Social Work series arose from a survey of BASW members to discover where they, the practitioners in social work, felt there was the most need for new literature. The response was overwhelming and enthusiastic, and the result is a carefully planned, coherent series of books. The emphasis is firmly on practice, set in a theoretical framework. The books will inform, stimulate and promote discussion, thus adding to the further development of skills and high professional standards. All the authors are practitioners and teachers of social work, representing a wide variety of experience.

JO CAMPLING

PRACTICAL SOCIAL WORK

Series Editor: Jo Campling

Social Work Practice

An Introduction

Veronica Coulshed

Foreword by Margaret Yelloly

MACMILLAN

First published 1988
Reprinted 1989, 1990

Published by
MACMILLAN EDUCATION LTD
Houndmills, Basingstoke, Hampshire RG21 2XS
and London
Companies and representatives
throughout the world

Printed in Hong Kong

British Library Cataloguing in Publication Data
Coulshed, Veronica
Social work practice: an introduction.
— (Practical social work).
1. Social service
I. Title II. Series
361.3   HV40
ISBN 0–333–45245–3 (hardcover)
ISBN 0–333–45246–1 (paperback)

To my mother

Series Standing Order

If you would like to receive future titles in this series as they are published,
you can make use of our standing order facility. To place a standing order
please contact your bookseller or, in case of difficulty, write to us at the
address below with your name and address and the name of the series.
Please state with which title you wish to begin your standing order. (If you
live outside the United Kingdom we may not have the rights for your area,
in which case we will forward your order to the publisher concerned.)

Customer Services Department, Macmillan Distribution Ltd,
Houndmills, Basingstoke, Hampshire, RG21 2XS, England.

Contents

Foreword

Social work is still a relatively new and aspiring profession. Along with an expanded and diversified role for both statutory and voluntary sectors in the 1970s came new responsibilities, new forms of training and a burgeoning literature. Yet although there are now many more books about social work we still depend heavily on work produced for a North American readership. This book fills a major gap for an international text covering the main models of social work practice which can serve as a reliable and comprehensive introduction.

Veronica Coulshed has many years of practice and teaching experience and is particularly well qualified to present the major theoretical approaches now in use. She believes that theory should inform practice, and expand and enrich the practitioner's understanding and capacity to act helpfully in situations which may have similarities but are always in some sense unique; models and theories can help to guide us through confusing and problematic reality, but can only aid and never replace the essentially personal response which lies at the heart of social work. Each of the approaches discussed here is the subject of a huge literature in its own right, but what renders this book distinctive is the distillation of complex theory into a succinct and readable account which is brought vividly to life in the case material.

The author's view of social work is a broad one; she rightly discusses not only casework and counselling but also social work in the context of families, groups and communities, and this breadth adds greatly to the book's appeal. Even experi-

viii

enced practitioners should find something new. Of course the reader will want to explore some paths more fully, and the comprehensive guide to further reading should help in this. A major aim of the book is to update practice and to give space to newer developments which reflect the range and diversity of practice now. It also builds upon the pointers to effective practice generated by a growing research tradition, for example focused time-limited approaches. But there are few certainties and no room for dogmatism; the author's message is that no social worker should be content with a single set of tools or a narrow view of practice. The hallmark of the good practitioner is flexibility, and the capacity to respond imaginatively to different people and problems in diverse and effective ways.

This excellent and comprehensive book, written with wisdom and informed by years of practice, makes more sense of theory than any I have read in recent years, and its clarity and freshness should make it a foundation text for every student of social work.

University of Stirling   MARGARET YELLOLY

Acknowledgements

I am indebted to the clients, practitioners and students whose work I have drawn on in the case examples. I would like to thank my husband for his criticisms of the first draft and his constant support and encouragement.

VERONICA COULSHED

Introduction

I have wanted to write this book for many years and for many reasons. Chief amongst these is my conviction that theory improves practice. After years of using only my own ideas, I began to read and try out those introduced here. I found that clients gained from my clearer thinking and deeper understanding of their difficulties. Also I was able to adapt my methods of helping to their needs rather than the other way around. However, condensing the material has been like trying to fit a gallon into a pint pot! Each of the social work practice approaches would fill many library shelves and the reader may find that I have not covered all the points he or she would have wished. Nevertheless I hope that the advantages of having one volume, which incorporates the main methods in a digestible form, outweigh any drawbacks.

My prime aim was to facilitate the application of theory to practice. Therefore, in most of the chapters, I have summarised the essential theoretical ideas; then I have applied them to case material drawn from students', colleagues' and my own work. My years in social work teaching have taught me that linking theory to practice is best achieved by providing concrete examples and following these with suggestions for further reading: for this reason, extensive references are given. My second aim was to update established approaches and to introduce newer ones, especially for experienced social workers. When they become practice teachers, they help students to link classroom learning to agency practice and so this collection will assist them. Possibly, in the years since such readers became professional-

1

ly qualified, the social work landscape will have changed dramatically. Social services departments and training courses have continued to cover generic and specialist roles and tasks, but there has been a rise and fall and there is currently renewed interest in critical (if not radical) thinking about what social workers should be doing. We have felt the impact of technology, unemployment, inner city unrest, major health concerns and cutbacks. Yet against this back-cloth we have been asked to meet almost unnervingly high expectations, particularly of competence and effectiveness. I hope that this text makes a small contribution to the reader's way of working.

Regretfully, yet realistically, one must concede that a slim volume cannot do justice to all these developments. In any case, this is a book about how to do the job rather than the what and why of social work. There is an abundant literature debating the philosophy, politics and critiques of practice (see Galper, 1980 and Timms, 1983). While I do not overlook the fact that poverty and oppression remain our largest problems, it is in the political arena where fundamental social change will have to take place. In the meantime I wish to emphasise that politics, alongside dimensions of race, class, gender, values, ethics and worker self-knowledge are fundamental to all the practice methods employed. Similarly, the organisa-tional dimension, the contexts within which we operate, are vital to the help we give, especially if the agency is the problem, but any discussion of specific managerial strategies for change also lies outside the scope of this introductory volume.

I have been deliberately selective in the approaches chosen for analysis, basing this on the question 'What do social workers need to do a good day's, or night's work?' Most approaches can be used in combination with one another; the only ones which rely on a competing view of man are the psychosocial and the behavioural and thus cannot be used simultaneously with the same person (although an example is quoted of a practitioner who changed from one to the other with a client). Eclecticism is all right as long as it is not haphazard (Dryden, 1984): clients are not helped by a collection of desperate remedies. The most important point is that if you are going to choose a particular method this must be determined by the problem; we must never make the problem fit the method.

The only real specialism in social work may be the problem itself and so I have avoided categorisation by client group, field of practice, setting or level of working. Some topics such as mental illness or child abuse warrant advanced study; some methods, such as building and servicing community organisations, deserve separate attention. Happily, Twelvetrees (1985) has done this. What I have tried to do is to tease out from our multiple roles and tasks components of skills and knowledge which can be transferred across situations.

In the case examples I hope that I have not conveyed the idea that social work is simple. There are many issues which are still to be agreed upon, such as applying theory to practice, which is discussed in Chapter One. Chapter Two covers the core skills of collecting information and making assessments. Chapter Three looks at communication skills, drawing broadly on counselling theories to show how we have to learn to relate to others interpersonally and organisationally. Thus, as well as the techniques of listening, understanding and responding, I explore negotiating, problem solving, prioritising and decision making skills.

Social workers deal with people and systems in crisis: some techniques and a theoretical framework for understanding crisis intervention are detailed in Chapter Four. A method of problem solving which can lend itself to many levels is task-centred work, reviewed in Chapter Five. Practitioners are more familiar with and therefore tend to use the ideas presented in these early chapters. The later chapters focus on approaches which may be viewed as specialist ones but my intention is that they become part of everyone's armoury of knowledge and skills.

Two major schools of thought, the psychosocial and the behavioural approach are explained in Chapters Six and Seven respectively. Both have been misconceived and criticised. Psychosocial methods are the oldest in social casework, seen by radicals as a form of policing, forcing people to adjust to the *status quo*. (Early caseworkers were actually condemned as subversive by the establishment of their day, whereas some of today's reformers have institutionalised their radicalism through ideology rather than action.) Behavioural methods have been used to manipulate people to make them conform, for example in some institutions, but I shall explore some of the latest therapies whose ethics are less dubious.

I look at working with families in Chapter Eight and while this could be viewed as an optional rather than a fundamental approach, it is included because the interactional or systems perspective on which it is based is relevant to most work. Chapter Nine introduces working with groups and explores different models and ways of coping with difficult situations. The final chapter questions the need for new approaches. Small-scale services are continually being invented; encouraging citizen partnership has begun to change the structure and the delivery of some services. Working with informal carers and settings and developing strategies for community empowerment and networking are considered, and some case examples drawn. Many of the chapters include frameworks which summarise the main ideas; I hope that these will be found useful in comparing one approach to another and in getting hold of the essential components of knowledge and skill.

1

Relating Theory to Practice: Some Dilemmas

Can theory improve practice or is social work mere common sense? Should social workers be able to offer a range of methods and styles of work in order to meet client need or should they simply be themselves? These questions are addressed in this chapter.

The relationship between theory and practice

Many students find it difficult to relate theory to practice. This might be because, as Davies (1984) suggests, teachers do not establish the links very clearly. Usually our training courses are not designed to integrate seminars, where social problems can be jointly analysed from a variety of perspectives by psychologists, sociologists, political scientists, lawyers, theologians, doctors and practitioners. Even if this were possible students would still have to choose between different points of view and then decide what to do to meet a client's unique needs in a specific situation at a particular time. Comments such as 'What has this got to do with practice?' may arise because social work has no knowledge base of its own. We have had to borrow most of our ideas from the social and behavioural sciences which give only general explanations of social life. These theories are also inconsistent and speculative and as a result the application of theory to practice has to be tentative and uncertain. Because topics like psychology and sociology offer contradictory explanations of human behaviour, arguments about the usefulness or hind-

5

rance of relying on social science may remain as unfinished business for some time to come.

My view is that knowledge derived from medicine, law, philosophy and the social sciences will aid your assessments, but if you are intent on finding a 'true' explanation which will aid your intervention, you will remain confused and disillusioned. Psychology has been more useful in the degree to which you can apply some of the theories, although a knowledge of social networks is begining to have an impact on practice, as the final chapter shows. In the meantime, if you are prepared to see theoretical contributions as ways of enriching your thinking and understanding, you will gain a broad framework of information through which you will recognise the complexities and possible causes of human suffering.

Sometimes theory and practice are viewed as being in conflict with one another. I see them as complementary halves, part of a reciprocal relationship, a never-ending circle, which encourages us to keep an open mind and thereby increases the chance that we will be able to offer an individualised, flexible approach to problem solving. The book by Hardiker and Barker (1981) demonstrates, through case studies, how to apply social science theories to your work. These authors and others (Evans, 1976; Smid and van Krieken, 1984) have distinguished between theories of practice, (which are really theories *for* practices) and practice theory, which is our concern. Practice theories, (which are more properly termed approaches, since they direct rather than predict) allow us to look at specific, usable ideas. Whether we recognise it or not, theory-less practice does not exist; we cannot avoid looking for explanations to guide our actions. In order to make sense of our everyday experiences, so that we can explain to ourselves and to others what we are doing and why, we have to turn to theory. Research has shown that agencies which profess not to use theory offer a non-problem-solving, drifting service (Corby, 1982).

If we evaluate our efforts we may be able to highlight and repeat successful strategies, thereby creating much needed knowledge. By formulating hypotheses which rest on the reflection 'If I do such and such, then this will happen', we become engaged in theory building. Despite much of our theory being homespun, in that it is derived from experience, this practice wisdom has contributed greatly to social work methods. People who can use their heart and head, who can combine the academic with the practical, will take social work beyond doing. Freire (1972) calls this ability to think and do 'praxis'; if we accept that social work is an intellectual activity, incorporating reading and research, we may be in a better position to liberate practice.

However, while we might agree that social work is 'scientific art' (Siporin 1975) we should not be trying to make it into an applied science. There is a growing compulsion to fulfil a scientific commitment and this could have negative consequences, as educators have long since warned (Germain, 1970). Exploring what is probably unknowable has misled some of our critics into a mistaken optimism that there are certainties which will be found if only we try a bit harder.

Going beyond common sense

There seem to be no bounds to the knowledge and skills required to do social work, despite the claim that, 'anyone with a kind heart can do it' (Olsen, 1986, quoting Gladstone). The list of our roles and tasks continues to grow: practitioners have to be therapists, managers, reformers, researchers, planners, teachers and protectors. We cannot be experts at everything, yet, as we have seen, we are beginning to be expected to understand the cause and cure for many social ills and prove that our methods work. Personal qualities such as self-understanding, curiosity, determination and an ability to get along with people are necessary, but not sufficient, conditions for productive practice (Jordan, 1984). We need a kind heart, common sense and uncommon sense (Gammack, 1982).

A lot of time is spent in giving tangible, immediate and practical help, but understanding does not stop at this level. Accurate assessment and close attention to the processes by which we give these services have been shown to improve the quality of what we have to offer (Goldberg *et al.*, 1970). A friend of mine, whose daughter had been suddenly paralysed, asked social services for a wheelchair. This he was promptly given, but he felt that no one tried to understand what this problem meant to him. Additionally, not all requests for help are 'visible' and it takes more than a common understanding to work with, say, children, who may not convey their needs in straightforward ways. We also work with those who have help thrust upon them; the majority of clients dealt with by British social services departments are unwillingly referred. Working as an uninvited guest with clients and organisations takes persuasive skills of a very high order. Using resistance to change as energy for change takes cleverness, creativity and even humour. (Cade (1982) argues that a loving sense of humour blends well with some life situations which are themselves incongruous and illogical.)

Developing a repertoire of methods and styles of work

It seems obvious that, if we have a variety of tools in our workbag, we are more able to offer a service which is determined by client need rather than our own. Matching client and worker would be the ideal, but a more realistic alternative would be to get to grips with a range of approaches and methods. However there may be worries that learning the tricks of the trade (Whan, 1983) could result in technocrats who are so dazzled by their own performance that they stop caring and use their manoeuvres in a disrespectful, gimmicky way. But every method is only as good as the person using it: anyone can make bad use of any art (Watzlawick, 1978).

It is mooted that workers use their own, idiosyncratic, predictable style, no matter what the needs of the case in hand or the practice method employed (A. G. Brown, 1977). I have found that some versatility can be gained through experience and regular execution of skills. For instance, at one time my style was what Walrond-Skinner (1976) would call 'reactive'. I listened and responded to interviews but could never conduct them. When I began to practise family interviewing and groupwork, having to think on my feet allowed me occasionally to be one step ahead rather than always trailing one step behind. I was also able to model myself on a co-worker who was comfortable being active and directive. He learned to slow down and thus we both extended our manner of relating to others.

It is not easy to vary one's style. Students complain that they are deskilled whenever we try out social work methods using role-play. Spontaneity and naturalness are temporily lost. The dilemma for the trainer is that 'being yourself' is agreed to be a good starting point (Hugman, 1977). Learning to combine this with a professional use of self (see Gammack, 1982) is a necessary development: a conscious application of theory to practice, (*post hoc* or otherwise) coupled with self-awareness can uphold the values of our profession and ensure accountability and some objectivity. Like dancing and piano playing, repetitive practice leads to the ownership of new behaviours which 'feel' right.

There is so much to be done in meeting common human needs that practitioners need to be able to cope with a wide range of duties, some of which are pleasant and rewarding; others are unpleasant and even frightening. There is a great deal of emphasis on acquiring sensitivity and a lot less attention given to the courage that social workers need. This is apparent when removing someone's child, taking a person into a mental hospital, challenging a team of staff who do not want to change or confronting a needy client with the news that there are no resources to relieve the situation. Having to be tough as well as tender, assertive as well as supportive are basic to the positions of power held by all professionals. We also carry the burden of society's ambiguous perception of 'doing good' and yet being unpopular because we deal with those who are scapegoated for being unable to cope.

This is not to suggest that the practice approaches included here will enable you to become 'all things to all people': as long as social services remain residual rather than part of a comprehensive coverage to enhance the development of people, many dilemmas and ambiguities will remain. But keeping an open mind about ways of helping, so that methods can be varied according to set goals, may increase the scope for client and worker satisfaction, as would a conscious attempt by the worker to go beyond just 'being yourself'.

2

Assessment: The Skills of Collecting, Analysing and Understanding Information

Assessments are both a process and a product of our understanding. Doing and making evaluations of situations are core social work skills. This chapter examines the nature of assessments and how they are made; I draw attention to the value of asking good questions, not only as a way of gathering information, but as a form of intervention in itself. The possibility of using computer-aided assessments is briefly considered before two models of assessment are applied to one case situation. In order to emphasise that all human suffering must be seen in a wide social context, both these models are based on a unitary or systems perspective. These ecological frameworks help us to keep in mind that while our everyday practice is concerned to alleviate individual, family, group or community difficulties, many of them are, in fact, structurally induced. I conclude by recognising the importance of keeping records and suggesting goal-oriented methods as one way of so doing.

What are assessments and how are they made?

Before social workers can intervene, they have to undertake and make assessments. These can be likened to a social study of people and/or situations. The kinds of information which are usually gathered include data about the following:

10

- referral and referrer
- client or situation
- the problem and its meaning for significant people
- historical facts, if these are related to current issues
- functioning of people, (social, psychological, medical, etc.)
- age, status, roles, behaviour patterns
- life cycle stage reached
- environment and informal networks
- finances, resources, strengths
- how the problem or situation has been previously handled
- other agencies involved, etc.

Siporin (1975) offers guidelines for conducting such a study, but his checklist would involve collecting a vast amount of material. I think that the skill in doing and making assessments lies in an ability to collect enough, but not too much, information. Frequently learners attempt to find out everything, asking more and more questions, thereby possibly becoming confused by an information overload. It is as well to remember that we will never know all there is to know about people and systems, since assessments are always dynamic and continuous and, in this sense, never complete. In some ways too they are never 'true' inasmuch as they reflect the perspective of the assessor: 'What you see depends on where you look'.

Sources of information usually include clients themselves, significant people in their network, readily available data from agencies or material that has been published. It is a pity, for instance, that so little use is made of research findings or practice papers as short cuts to knowledge. Similarly, statistics are rarely consulted, although caution is recommended when reading some records or statistics ('State-istics' as McNeill (1985) calls them!).

The major purpose of assessments is to gain knowledge and understanding of people and circumstances so as to predict and guide intervention. They are sometimes called appraisals or 'diagnostic formulations' which can describe, explain, predict, evaluate, (situations not people) and prescribe: they often help organisations to certify eligibility for services and can assist in planning and deciding policy. Assessments are both short- and long-term: for instance, a short-term assessment will provide immediate protection for an abused child, but a long-term assessment will assess the prospects for rehabilitation and offer alternatives and realistic plans.

Accuracy is vital, especially when gathering material evidence. One way of aiming for this might be to gather data systematically, rather than in a random fashion; also to cross-check information where possible and not to rely on hearsay or gossip. Another way of ensuring accuracy is to share your assessment with the subject of the study: if client and worker jointly undertake this exercise, it becomes an interactional process which could lead to a more open partnership. I notice that staff in some children's homes like to write their reports together with the children so that recording too is open (Doel and Lawson, 1986). (In any case, I always record my assessments as if the client is looking over my shoulder.) Currently, some assessments are one-way and serve only the worker's purpose: where they can be shared, this could be the start of change and the basis for an honest exchange.

Similarly, self-assessments can be informative to those who undertake them. While bureaucratic procedures might dictate data collection on standardised agency pro-formas and review sheets, my work with an adoption and fostering team has shown how even their forms can be completed by the families themselves: they see this as an enjoyable task, giving a brief resumé of themselves and their lifestyle and interests. These 'pen pictures' are useful sources of information to all the parties involved.

It is essential that appraisals emphasise strengths and resources and do not focus only on what is wrong. Unfortunately, social work assessments continue to include a large number of negative labels, such as 'inadequate parent' or 'aggressive personality': (in fact, research has shown that name-calling increases the longer a person is 'socialised' into our profession; see Case and Lingerfelt, 1974). The avoidance of negative assessments may lie partly in treating every day in the job as your first, inasmuch as you learn to monitor your tendency to become 'case-hardened' or cynical. I remember having to do this after several stressful years in a busy hospital social work department: I found that I was responding impatiently to callers at the door as if they were nuisances. Many people required redirecting elsewhere but I occasionally failed to assess when the person needed more help than just this. Job stress can affect the clear judgement of others and can eventually lead to professional 'burn out' (Zastrow, 1984).

To recapitulate: an assessment is a perceptual/analytic process of selecting, categorising, organising and synthesising data: it is both a process and a product of our understanding. This social study avoids labels and is reached as a result of logical analysis of data which has been carefully and systematically collected. Priority is given to the participants' own view of their situation. However, social work also deals with feelings, metaphorical communications, intuition and interpretation: thus, professional judgements cannot be reached quite so straightforwardly. We will always make mistakes whatever our own Utopian ideals and the sometimes impossible reforms advocated by those who criticise us: ironically, the Beckford Inquiry accused social workers of misplaced optimism yet sought to suggest that mistakes should not be made (*A Child in Trust*, 1985).

There are ways in which you could reduce the risk of error or bias in your assessments and these will be noted, before I go on to tasks which might be undertaken. As previously suggested, you can:

1. Cross-check assessments with clients, their network, colleagues and available data.

2. Try to be self-aware and monitor when you are trying to normalise or rationalise data as to make your formulation come true.

3. Beware of being too much in awe of those who hold higher status or power: a person in authority may not be an authority. An over-readiness to accept their views could lead to distorted reasoning and perception. I have described elsewhere how a child abuse case conference had to be strategically managed to avoid mistakes of this kind (Coulshed and Abdullah-Zadeh, 1985).

4. Treat all assessments as working hypotheses which

ought to be substantiated by further knowledge. Remember that they are essentially speculations derived from objective and subjective sources. The social work processes involved in formulating assessments have been seen by Curnock and Hardiker (1979) as follows:

Phase 1 – Making contact
Phase 2 – Building relationships and liaising with agencies
Phase 3 – Using relationships and becoming a client

In each of these phases, the worker attempts to build up a picture which will guide intervention by collecting information from as many significant sources as possible; from this basis an attempt is made to reach an evaluation of the circumstances. Then the balance between need, risks and resources is clarified and goals for intervention identified.

The same authors have applied their framework to the particular example of preparing a report for the court. This is essentially an assessment of the person and the context in which an alleged offence occurred, from which a recommendation for disposal is offered. Thus it is a document which has to take into account due process, justice and welfare. Hardiker and Curnock (1984) demonstrate that information gathering and understanding the meaning of events can be complex and time-consuming. We have to beware of doing social inquiry reports on an assembly line basis, if we are to ensure that an optimum assessment document is produced.

The same attention to detail is fundamental to the assessment of children in care who are awaiting permanency planning (Maluccio *et al.*, 1986) On the basis of a social study into their lives, the decision is made whether or not they should live outside their homes with new families. In my judgement this task is so important that a team of people could be involved in the process. Everyone who knows anything about the child can contribute. One social worker, faced with an eleven-year-old boy who had been in care for most of his life, first of all read his file carefully.From this she constructed a flow chart diagram showing his numerous moves from one caretaker to another. She noted that there ᵃre gaps in his history, which can happen if records are not ᵗy kept. However, from the available information, she, a student and the key worker in the small children's home where the boy lived set out to interview as many people as possible who had had contact with him. They also took photographs of places and of anyone significant in his history.This is a common way of starting a life story book (Maluccio *et al.*, 1986), but in this case the information was also needed to make an assessment of the child's attachments in the past, so that his capacity to make new attachments in the future could be evaluated.

As with other assessments, formal tools for measuring such things as attachment, bonding, stage of development reached, self-image and so on were used to supplement the information gained from direct work with the child. Numerous games and exercises were undertaken with the boy by the key worker and student, so that they could let him gradually open the door to his past, often reliving his grief in order to resolve it to allow for new relationships. The quality of his relationships with these helpers and his ability to talk about his losses were vital components in the assessment.

Interviewing and the ability to ask 'good' questions

In most social work texts, the purpose of interviewing is viewed less as a means of helping and more a way of collecting data to aid assessment and understanding. In the interview we observe, participate and ask questions. We may assume that the ability to ask questions can be taken for granted. But, if we are to gather relevant information, we have to anticipate the kind of answer which a particular question will provoke. Equally, if we want the process of questioning to benefit the person and introduce new information or perspectives, then we have to become skilled at asking 'good' questions. If we do so, this can become a valuable technique which can be used as a form of intervention as well as just eliciting information.

For example, the technique of circular questioning is used by family therapists in order to assess family interaction (Penn, 1982). This is mentioned again in Chapter Eight and involves asking one member of the family to comment on the relationship or behaviour of two other members. Thus, 'When your mother tries to get Andrew to go to school, what does your grandmother do?' and, 'Who do you think is closer to your father, your sister or your brother?' and so on. This procedure achieves a number of things: it provides new information for the family group who may never have actually heard this perspective; it links one person to another, showing how people relate, and it highlights the differences between people. (You could use this technique with any group or even in individual interviews where you are trying to assess interpersonal problems.)

As well as using questionnaires, surveys, self-perception tests, rating scales, problem checklists, sentence completion and role-play exercises, the book by Priestley *et al.* (1978) recommends the use of the journalist's standby – the '5WH Test'. This is a formula for asking questions such as who, what, when, where, why and how? A blend of sentences beginning with any of these will uncover a lot of basic information. For example, 'What is the problem; when did it start; how have you tried to cope; who could help; where should we be aiming in sorting things out?' and so on. I would caution against the too ready use of 'Why?' in making such enquiries: it promotes an abrupt interrogative style, could put people on the defensive and might block a more revealing answer. A student recently asked an elderly person why she had been afraid to go out; a more productive question might have been, 'What do you think might have happened if you had gone out?' (A fascinating book which will promote rapport through skilful use of questioning and help others to reveal to themselves the depth of their experiences is *The Sructure of Magic* by Bandler and Grinder, 1975.)

Other practitioners have written about the usefulness of asking questions in order to raise consciousness (Henderson and Thomas, 1980). In neighbourhood work the fieldworker could use, besides the reporter type of questions, a more challenging devil's advocate type of approach: here the respondent is deliberately confronted with the argument of opponents in order to trigger change. Other 'posing' questions include hypothetical ones, such as, 'What if . . .?' or asking someone to describe the ideal. For example, I worked with a family whose twelve-year-old boy was referred by the GP because of 'dizzy spells' for which no physical cause had been found. His baby sister had recently died and he had never cried. I asked him, 'Who would get more upset if you got upset, your mum or your grandmother?' (his carers). He replied that it would be his mother, thereby giving me, and the family, a clue to further work. On another occasion I asked a thirteen-year-old girl, the youngest of four children who had not attended school for a year, 'What if your mum decided to leave your father, who would she take with her?' This was always threatened by the mother who agreed that this child would be the one she would take: the hypothetical and 'What if?' suggestions can bring out important themes for people to consider.

In community self-help groups, these kinds of problem-posing questions are preferable to those used by self-appointed leaders, who 'invade' others with ready answers, rather than promote dialogue for learning (Randall and Southgate, 1980). An example of allowing groups to assess their own ideas was given by a student who had been a member of an unemployed group. In reply to a despairing remark, 'It's useless, we can't get them to change their policies' the student explored, 'Who are *they*; what do we know of their policies?'

To summarise: the main way we make assessments is by asking questions; experts can show us how to use this technique as a way of saving time, engaging the interviewee rather than alienating through 'interrogation' and as a tool for actually beginning to change a situation.

Computer-aided assessments

If medicine is anything to go by, new technology may help us in the future in making social diagnoses. The use of computers is proving a worthwhile, if underused, resource (Glastonbury, 1985). On project which exploits computer technology is called the FAM (Family Assessment Measure) programme. It is described below, before we move on to a case example which illustrates the conventional systems approach to undertaking assessments.

Some researchers are helping families in difficulty by

asking individual members to answer computer-posed questions; subsequently the results are analysed from an individual, dyadic and collective relationships standpoint. The FAM programme can handle all this information and goes beyond describing the family structure to analysing the family's functioning: for instance, it explores how tasks are accomplished, roles performed, control used, communication patterns adopted, affection used and the norms and values held. Each member receives a print-out of this information, prior to meeting the family worker who may use this information to guide or confirm assessments (Steinhauer, 1984).

I have been using these self-report questionnaires manually to help foster care workers to select and prepare prospective families for their future roles. Thus far the results confirm that families' and workers' assessments, made in the usual way beforehand, agree with the results obtained from the FAM questionnaires.

A case example using two models of assessment

The following referral was analysed by a student in placement, using two models of assessment. The first is an adaptation of that suggested by Vickery (1976) while the second explores the model put forward by Forder (1976). These unitary or systems approaches have been used by professional training courses over the past few years and, despite some criticism (Langan, 1985) seem to offer the best analytical frameworks thus far available to us.

These were initial assessments, the start of the student's thinking through of the situation. Reading about the Kent Community Care Scheme (Challis and Davies, 1985) had alerted the learner to the cost-effectiveness of keeping elderly people in their own homes if they wish. Thus the assessment of the client Mr R and the systems affecting him takes into account that residential accommodation costs more than full-time domiciliary services. (Unfortunately, flexible choices which allow for care at home are not widely available to elderly people.) Some of the goals may look unrealistic given that:

1. Referrals for assessment are often made after decisions for 'disposal' have already been made.
2. Some of the action plans would require long term effort, whilst the referral is for a rapid solution.
3. The roles and tasks for the worker appear daunting.

Referral 'Mr R, 86 years old, feels he is unable to care for himself at home once he leaves hospital. He lives alone in a quiet suburb, visited only by his next door neighbours and his vicar. Mr R needs 'meals-on-wheels' and home help but the service cannot be given over the weekend. The neighbours are willing to help but say that Mr R has frequent falls and may be at some risk: he himself would prefer to enter a home as he is lonely and no longer wants the responsibility of his house. There are no immediate vacancies in the Local Authority hostel and since the hospital needs the bed, Mr R has decided to enter a private nursing home; after visiting it, he is unhappy that it is so large and so far from his own locality.'
Vickery (1976) asks:

1. What are the problems in this situation?
2. Who are the clients (i.e. those who will benefit)?
3. What are the goals?
4. Who has to be changed or influenced?
5. What are the tasks and roles of the social worker?

These questions have to be answered at the level of the individual, the group, the neighbourhood, the organisation and the wider environment. The assets and liabilities in the situation are:

1. Mr R is physically and mentally well at the moment.
2. He is popular on the ward and enjoys company.
3. He adjusts well to change and has coped with the crisis of admission to hospital following a fall.
4. There is pressure from the hospital to discharge him.
5. The local authority resources are inadequate.
6. Community network resources are undeveloped.

For an adaption of the Vickery model, see Table 2.1.
The same problem definitions will emerge using the model outlined by Forder (1976), much simplified to show that it is

Table 2.1　*Initial assessment*

Definition of the problem	Client	Goals	Target	Role/task of social worker
Mr R's inability and uncertainty about living alone	Mr R	Obtain hostel/ nursing home place	Mr R	Enabler Resource finder/broker
Undeveloped community networks/ resources	Mr R and local people	Persuade social services department and voluntary agencies to start care schemes	Social Services Department Voluntary Groups Community leaders, etc.	Educator Planner Budgeter Advocacy Research Public relations
Lack of community care services and hostel places Policy regarding private care	Social service department clients	Review policies regarding home help, meals on wheels etc. Increase vacancies	SSD committee and managers Department of Health and Social Security	Presenter of case for policy change and increased spending on elderly clients
Pressure on hospital beds	Medical staff	Review discharge procedures	Hospital and Department of Health and Social Security	Researcher Campaigner Negotiator

not necessary to understand or study general system theory itself. Here one first names the different systems involved in the problem; see for instance Figure 2.1.

Then each system and each person is analysed in terms of:

1. Information, values and knowledge.
2. Resources, including skills and coping.
3. Goals.
4. Power.
5. Communication within and between them.
6. External systems which interact with them.
7. The stage of development (life cycle).
8. Morale.

These models can also suggest where changes in the relationships between the various systems are needed, for example where communication needs to be improved or where goals are incongruent. The limitations of the models are that they do not prescribe specific action: this depends on many factors which include the client's wishes, the worker's power, agency constraints and the time available.

In concluding this section, I would not want to subscribe to the notion that our assessments, that is our problem definitions, should be 'shaped by what we think we can do' (Siporin, 1975, p. 244). Rather assessments should describe situations from a broadened perspective, otherwise we will not move outside the boundaries given to us: critical thinking can lead to the development of more responsive types of services. Our assessments are the start of this.

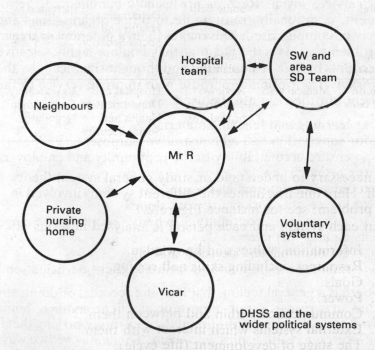

Figure 2.1 *Diagram based on Forder's model of assessment*

Keeping records

Although seen as a troublesome chore, recording is an essential part of social work practice and is a major skill. The record registers significant facts, evidence, judgements and decisions and explains the actions taken. It may take the form of a detailed verbatim account or a summary of each incident or contact, with periodic, analytical or interpretive sections. It summarises the intake, continuing and closing phases of work, evaluating the progress made. The record might also hold transfer summaries from previous workers, forms, letters, documents and reports by other agencies, even transcripts from audio or videotape material, and possibly a social history.

Social workers often make personal records or jot down notes, usually in their diary. These need to be distinguished from records for agency purposes which are official registers of services given. Records are usually confidential, permanent, occasionally transferable to other organisations and may be computerised. This makes them a potential source of problems, as does the fact that they contain highly selective accounts of data remembered and thought significant by the worker. Their primary purpose is to improve service to the client but they can also be used:

- as learning and teaching material
- for supervision and administrative purposes
- to ensure accountability to the community and employers
- for research
- to advocate reforms and resources
- to 'cover' the worker for work done
- to provide continuity when workers change
- as an *aide mémoire*
- to aid planning and decision making
- to monitor progress and to facilitate client participation.

There is a general feeling that keeping records, or doing any kind of writing, is not important as client contact. Some workers feel guilty writing about their clients, worrying that it interferes in relationships with them. There may be two ways of combating this. Firstly, by further standardising recording forms we might cut down the time involved. Giving clear, concise, accurate, objective and up-to-date accounts of work done is a disciplined skill. I find that some practitioners are unable or unwilling to edit their reports, misguidedly equating lengthy recordings with greater commitment and a higher quality of work. Mastering the use of a dictaphone saves time, if reports are typed later. Secondly, client access to records should increase their power over what is recorded about them. One study showed that clients have a strong interest in sharing the record keeping, negotiating with their helpers about what is put down at the end of each interview or contact (Doel and Lawson, 1986).

Some methods of social work, especially Task-Centred Work (see Chapter Five) call for work by contract, relying on the worker's willingness to become more accountable to the client and perhaps share the account of the work done. Writing the report together is simpler if it is a goal-oriented record, requiring thinking and writing in four major areas. These are:

1. *What is the problem?* This should be as explicit as possible; for example, in the previous case example. 'Mr R does not wish to continue living in his own home. There is pressure on hospital beds. He wishes to enter residential accommodation in his own locality. Available private homes are large and too far away for visitors. There is no vacancy in the authority's home.'

2. *What are the strengths and resources?* for example, 'Mr R is well at the moment. He enjoys company. He coped with his admission to hospital. He has friends and neighbours who would visit him in an elderly persons' home.'

3. *What are the goals?* 'The hospital procedures for emptying beds will be discussed at the next ward round. If Mr R must go home maximum services will need to be provided. A local hostel or nursing home place will be obtained and Mr R's name is on the list.'

4. *What is the plan?* 'To discuss with the client the range of possible solutions and enable him to find and use available and potential resources. To present the case for policy change to the social services department regarding the research into

comparative costs of keeping elderly people at home with services or paying supplements towards nursing home care. To check with the medical and nursing staff what their plans are.'

Where social work can be task-focused, systematic record keeping is made easier. The details which can be included are:

Case number and name
Date opened and last reviewed
Practical services and changes planned and given
Problems tackled and remaining
Outside agencies in contact with worker and client
Major changes which will be aimed for
Time before case is likely to be closed
Social worker efforts
Client efforts towards problem resolution, and so on.

3

Counselling and Other Ways of Influencing for Change

Social work is concerned with influencing people and achieving change. We do this by using interpersonal and organisational skills. The word 'counselling' has been chosen to cover both these levels of activity. We communicate and relate to people by observation, listening and responding; accompanying these tasks are those of problem solving, decision making and negotiating with, and on behalf of, clients. It is these areas which this chapter explores.

What is counselling?

There has been a great deal of debate about definitions of counselling (Nelson-Jones, 1983). I will use the term broadly to encompass the client-centred approach of Rogers (1980), the problem solving model prescribed by Egan (1981) and the very wide way in which the Barclay Committee described what social workers do, namely, 'counselling and social care planning' (Barclay, 1982). This will allow us to consider the various methods of influencing and attempting to bring about change. Counselling incorporates the notions of relationship, skill, and different kinds of aims: we engage in crisis, developmental, problem-solving and supportive counselling interviews. At the same time we can differentiate counselling according to the theoretical orientation of the worker, so that there are behavioural, psychodynamic and humanistic counsellors. Whatever our aims or theoretical stance, the fundamental skills of observing, listening and responding remain. They are at the heart of helping. Mastery of them is far from simple; even experienced practitioners continue to learn.

So what does it take to become a skilled counsellor? A blend of being good at human relations and being a technical expert is favoured by Nelson-Jones (1983). The former quality belongs to a person who cares and who not only understands people but who can show this. Self-knowledge and self-acceptance are essential prerequisites – counselling is a two-way process affecting worker and client: the latter elicits as well as expresses feelings (Kell and Mueller, 1966). Within this reciprocal whole a vulnerable or defensive counsellor will find it difficult to help someone whose self-concept and protective defence mechanisms have become part of the problem.

Inventory of counselling skills

There are a growing number of books available to help develop technique, offering many exercises for practice, and these need not be repeated here (Egan, 1977). Instead it may be more useful to concentrate on some of the common errors and areas of special difficulty which learners seem to encounter. I have documented below a checklist drawn from teaching these micro skills so that readers can identify where they may have limitations and accordingly need to focus their efforts. I confess my own 'sticking-points' at the end of the list!
Are you able to:

Let a person finish talking without reacting?
Accurately reflect back content and feelings?
Paraphrase what someone has said?
Summarise to move interviews forward?
Clarify your own role to the other person?
Use open questions?
Use minimal prompts to encourage person to go on?
Watch for non-verbal cues?

Draw out feelings?
Offer tentative understanding?
Tune in to how the other person affects you?
Tolerate silences of about five seconds?
Control your own anxiety and relax?
Relate genuinely to the other person?
Focus on the 'here and now'?
Provide direction and keep focus in interviews?
Focus on the person's strengths?
Offer alternative perspectives on problems?
Time and pace the flow of the interview?
Draw out concrete examples of the difficulties?
Recognise and confront ambivalence, inconsistency?
Set mutual goals?
Help formulate plans for change?
Discuss and generate alternatives?
Clarify to aid the other's self-understanding?
Tolerate painful topics?
Evaluate costs and gains in solutions reached?
Prepare someone for the end of an interview?

I 'get stuck' with the first two skills, mainly, I think, because of my teaching experience, which allows for a lot of guidance and information giving. This is all right, providing direction and advice are offered when it is timely to do so. It is generally unhelpful to talk from my own perspective whenever I am interviewing, yet I hear myself saying, for example, 'I think . . .' or 'My feelings are . . .' By talking about 'me' and 'my' I fail to enter the other person's frame of reference, which is what really matters. Responses need not be cleverly thought out when situations are still being explored: frequently all that is needed is to reflect back the other's statements using 'You think . . .' or 'Your feelings are . . .' This is a technique which *lets people listen to themselves* – a rare luxury nowadays.

There are other barriers to active listening, accurate observation and empathic response. These include working with people who are of a different class, race or gender; receiving angry or complimentary feedback; talking about topics such as sex; anxiety about inexperience; feeling responsible for people's problems; initial interviews and what Jacobs (1985) calls, 'having two mouths and one ear'! Unhelpful styles are those which are preaching, interpretive, evaluative, over-directive or falsely reassuring. In sum, not allowing the other person to be different from oneself. If you check your own behaviour, audiotape your work or practise with a colleague, you may discover tendencies that you would wish to change.

Two counselling models

Before a case example is used to show the theory in action, a framework for understanding *Rogers' client-centred approach* (1980) is outlined below, in summary form.

Theory base and important concepts are elements from humanistic psychology, which is concerned with growth and 'becoming': an optimistic, existential view of man, which recognises the importance of the self concept and self-actualisation in becoming a 'fully functioning person'. In order to achieve this, relationships with significant others require unconditional positive regard, empathy, authenticity, and warmth. The theory draws on phenomenology, the way in which the person's experience of their self is congruent or otherwise with the way they 'experience their self in the world.'

Problems which arise include psychological disturbance due to the inner conflict between self-experience and the way one is perceived by others: conditional acceptance from important people limits the extent to which one can really be oneself.

Goals of therapy are to assist someone to become fully functioning, to gain congruence between inner experience and the outer self via a relationship which is accepting, unconditional, genuine and non-possessive.

The client's role is to move away from 'oughts' and 'shoulds', that is, living up to the expectations of others. The person moves towards becoming 'real, honest, self-accepting with a here-and-now experiencing of self'; that is the person learns to define her/himself rather than accepting the views of others.

The worker's role and techniques. Rogers would say that there are no techniques as such; much depends on the self-acceptance of the worker who can then accept others in a warm, genuine, empathic relationship. The therapist provides a facilitative, non-directive climate in which the client's feelings can be accurately reflected. Reaching for feelings may be necessary if these are not stated, along with mirroring them, pacing, clarifying, summarising them and the way in which the client expresses them. The worker must be able to convey understanding: by caring, in a non-possessive way, the worker allows the person to begin to care for her/his self.

Case example

Linda is sixteen, living at home with her mother who is a single parent. There are two older children, grown up and living away from home. Linda attends the local Technical College, studying a business course. She calls in at the office of the social services to ask for help. She feels desperate because her mother is asking her to help with the housework, leaving little time for Linda to study for her exams which are looming.

The transcript is taken from the first interview in the first half hour of which the client unloads all of her mixed-up feelings towards her mother and her *self*. Her mother, burdened by her own duties, tells Linda that she is selfish and lazy. About half an hour into the meeting, with the counsellor, Linda was relaxed but still confused about her relationship to her mother.

L (despairingly) I can't do anything to please my mum.
C How does that make you feel?
L (after a pause) I don't know.
C You look sad about it.
L Well, it makes me feel miserable . . . (struggling)
C . . . Not knowing what pleases your mother?
L Nothing I do pleases her.
C Are you saying that the things you do for your mother are not appreciated? Is that what makes you feel miserable?

L   I just wish she would not keep picking on me. I would do anything for her but she only wants it done in her time.

C   Can you give me an example of something that has happened this week?

L   Yes. This morning she asked me to do the breakfast dishes. I was late for 'Tech' and said I'd do them when I got home. But she ranted and raved so I had to do them then.

C   You sound angry about that.

L   I think she is being unreasonable.

C   (neutral tone) You feel *you're* not unreasonable

L   *She* says I am.

C   What do you think?

L   About not doing the dishes?

C   Yes. Do you feel that you are unreasonable as a person?

L   I don't know.

Acceptance may have been witheld by a continued repetition of 'If you don't do the housework, you don't care about me.' Linda might have heard an implication that 'You are therefore a bad person and I don't love you.' This is a kind of conditional acceptance of another person. We also tend to internalise other's opinions of us, which can alienate us from valuing ourselves: Noonan (1983) writes that interaction with significant others encourages an infant to learn to differentiate 'organismic' experiences into 'me' and 'not me' phenomena.

In the interview, the worker is helping Linda to work towards a reflective re-cognition of herself, separate from the way others apparently see her. (I have found that this conflict can be at the root of many difficulties where clients become depressed and confused about who they really are.) No blame is apportioned and it is vital to empathise with all parties in the situation. (Further contact may or may not involve the family, depending on the wishes of the client.)

This approach may be scorned by workers who say that Social Services have no time for allowing people to work things out for themselves. This book explores many of the other avenues for helping, but it would be short-sighted to dismiss any of the methods on the grounds that they do not work or there is no time. Feeling supported while exploring one's ambivalent feelings can motivate people towards self-management rather than having to return to our departments time and again.

Another useful counselling model is the three-stage model attributed to Egan (1981), although recently at a conference he extended this to a fourth stage where evaluation takes place. He represents the four stages of *Exploration, Understanding, Action and Review* by four adjacent diamond shapes; these signify the widening and narrowing of focus within each interview and throughout the whole helping process. Thus following a wide exploration of the problem the worker helps the client to narrow down their discussion so that an assessment can be formulated; following this the interview opens up again so that client and helper can gain a thorough understanding and perhaps a new perspective of the difficulties and therefore the specific goals to aim for; in order to consider what to do to achieve the change the interview has to be wide-ranging again so that alternatives can be considered prior to focusing down on a particular plan; when reviewing, 'how did it go?' space is offered to broadly evaluate the chosen strategy and perhaps return to the first stage again in a circular process of helping. Some skills which can be used in each stage are as follows:

Stage One: exploration skills The social worker aims to establish a rapport with the client and, by using appropriate responses, assists in the exploration of thoughts, feelings and behaviour relevant to the problem in hand. Asking, 'What is the difficulty?' the helper starts to build trust and a working alliance by using active listening, reflecting, paraphrasing and summarising skills. Open questions are used before the client is asked to say specifically and concretely which problem they and the worker need to try to understand.

Stage Two: understanding skills The worker continues to be facilitative, using stage one skills and additionally, trying to help the person to piece together the picture that has emerged, seeing, possibly, themes and patterns with regard to which the helper can offer a new perspective. This alternative point of view aids clearer understanding of what the person's goals are and identifies strengths and resources which would help the situation. The skills lie in offering an alternative frame of reference, using appropriate self-disclosure, staying in touch with what is happening here-and-now and in the use of confrontation to challenge inconsistencies or conflicting ideas. Timing and pacing are essential to know when to confront and when to support.

Stage Three: action skills The worker and client begin to identify and develop resources for resolving or coping with the causes for concern, using this thorough understanding of self and situation. The skills lie in setting goals, providing support and resources, teaching problem solving if appropriate, agreeing the contract and purpose of meeting and using decision-making abilities.

Stage Four: review An action plan having been chosen and tried, the ideas are reviewed. The worker's skills revert to active listening and those of all the previous stages.

Structuring the initial sessions: a four-stage plan

Another way of illustrating the beginning, middle and ending phases of contacts is shown in Table 3.1 adapted from Nelson-Jones (1983).

The social worker's use of influence and authority

Not all clients are willing or ask for help and counselling skills include setting limits, taking charge in a crisis, and using legal powers responsibly. We serve as agents of social control, rationers of scarce resources and modifiers of social policy (Pincus and Minahan, 1973). Our authority stems not only from agency function and statutory powers and duties, but from professional qualifications, personal credibility, the strength of our persuasiveness and the quality of our relationships. We have to remember, though, that we are only as powerful as people allow us to be: our influence has to be validated by clients and others. Frequently we have to

Table 3.1 *Initial sessions: phases and tasks*

1. BEGINNING	'Meeting, greeting, seating' (Nelson-Jones, 1983)
	Establish confidentiality and its limitations
	Start to build rapport and trust and begin data collection
2. THE PROBLEM	Help the person to talk
	Explore current worries and concerns
	Assist in amplifying, clarifying and specifying particular difficulties
3. RELATING	Structure the pace and timing of the interview
	Broaden an exploration of the bio-psycho-social aspects
	Assist further exploration, clarification and client self-disclosure
	Worker self-disclosure where appropriate
4. CONTRACTING and ENDING	Summarise the interview so far
	Structure prior to ending
	Formulate and discuss goals
	Present helping methods
	Handle questions
	Agree goals, methods and tasks
	Clarify administration details
	Arrange the next meeting
	Parting

Adapted from Nelson-Jones, 1983.

convince people that we can help. There is a need to counteract resistance to 'the welfare'. Dale *et al.* (1986) have produced helpful ways of using power and influence, as part of their role as NSPCC inspectors working with families, which are worth studying.

There are ways, too, of sharing authority and influence with our users. One project helped long-term clients to regain control over their lives by sharing professional knowledge and authority; poor families were encouraged to take over the decision making, resources and relationships with their workers who delegated power, partnering their previously dependent clients as they moved towards real citizen control of services (Benn, 1981). These ideas are developed in Chapter Ten.

Other ways of influencing for change: negotiation skills

It is surprising to find that we negotiate all the time; for example, arranging meetings, sorting out rules with teenagers and so on. It is also part of our daily, professional practice to persuade schools to cope with disruptive pupils, induce policy makers to fund projects, or liaise with community networks on behalf of mentally handicapped people. Additionally, as problems of poverty loom larger on everyone's workloads, the skilled use of advocacy and negotiation is fundamental. To be a skilled negotiator the core requirements for competence in communication and interpersonal relating remain; without careful observation, listening and understanding, there is no scope for getting to know the other's point of view, for helping them to understand yours nor for ensuring that everyone knows what the objectives are.

One of my colleagues illustrates some of the extra qualities needed: prior to meetings where changes are to be proposed, she pre-negotiates with individuals, plans a campaign to deal with setbacks and anticipates the implications for others of her suggestions. It appears that self-awareness is also invaluable for realising how one is perceived by others, for being alert to the impact one is having and for ensuring control of one's own reactions. Being seen as a realist who is constructive, willing to compromise and preferring cooperation to confrontation helps one to reach agreements that will stick (Axelrod, 1984).

Of course there are specific, behavioural manoeuvres which can be used when influencing for change. These include making clear proposals and suggestions; building on these and any support offered by other people, summarising the position reached in order to test for understanding, and being seen to be 'generous' by the other party. A leaflet published by the Industrial Society (1981) advises also against defending oneself, stating difficulties, attacking and making excuses (rather than being open about being wrong).

To summarise: the skills of an expert negotiator are listening, talking persuasively, understanding self and others, dealing with process and content, using tactics and planning. These seem to be relevant tools for social workers, who are frequently trying to get others to do something. A 'pushy' style of negotiating, which is one-way and only gives, rather than seeks information is less likely, in the long term, to get commitment to a course of action (Laborde, 1983). For instance, before I could introduce much needed changes in an elderly persons' home so as to improve the quality of life for the residents, I had to spend a lot of time asking the care staff what *they* wanted to improve job satisfaction. In my first meeting with the staff, therefore, I asked them to note down on cards the answers to 'What are the problems here for you?' and 'What talents do you have to overcome these?' (Coulshed, 1980). This information was shared in the session and formed the basis for negotiating changes which would benefit the residents and staff alike.

Problem-solving and decision-making skills

Another skill that we practise all the time is solving problems and choosing between alternative courses of action. As soon as you look into your in-tray for the day you begin to do this: you see that an elderly person is applying for a telephone because of her isolation and frailty; another client has been delivered of her baby which is to be placed for adoption; a further task is for you to arrange for a person who is mentally handicapped to see a small group home in the community where he may eventually live. Accordingly, you plan your diary for the morning, but on the way out a homeless man asks if you can find him accommodation. . ... How you allocate your time and priorities involves a capacity for problem solving and decision making.

At this point you could refer back to Egan's helping model, as this shows the stages for problem solving, but the intention now is to explore briefly how the human mind works, in order to improve your problem-solving capacities and so that you can teach this skill to others (Perlman, 1957).

The first job is to ascertain and clarify the facts, (these include what the problem 'means' to those involved). If you go about this in an orderly way, ignoring irrelevancies, then overwhelming difficulties may be cut down to manageable size. Confusion can be lessened further by 'thinking through' as a next step: this involves going over the problem in your mind, looking for connections and patterns of 'what may have caused what', considering possible actions you could take and the consequences, separating what is important from what is less so and imagining ways of coping or adapting. The third step is to develop alternative plans for action: if freedom to think clearly has been made possible by lowering anxiety, then space for creating solutions will have been generated. The fourth phase is to make choices based on 'What if I do?' and 'How will I manage if I don't?', bearing in mind any constraints and resources.

If you look again at your in-tray referrals, you will see that these processes and the decisions you reach are based mainly on value judgements. How you plan your workload is influenced by a valuing process of deciding which clients' needs ought to have priority. The final stage of problem solving is to look back on the action taken and review the outcome in readiness for the next time. To summarise: when we are defining problems we are mainly analytical; when generating solutions we are mainly imaginative and when choosing solutions we are essentially evaluative (Adair, 1976).

Taking key decisions, for instance whether or not to take away a person's liberty or implementing a Quality Assurance programme, usually generates a set of options involving numerous factors which have to be weighed; values, as well as knowledge are implied here and these have to be revealed, otherwise treatment decisions are likely to be inconsistent, of a low standard and contradictory (Algie, 1986). Algie's research and computer programme, Priority Decision Systems (PDS), has apparently improved the level of agreement and consistency within teams working on child abuse procedures. The same programme has been used by magistrates to examine their sentencing decisions.

There could be drawbacks to building models which try 'scientifically' to evaluate complex factors, so as to aid decisions. Real life does not offer a static picture, neither is it only concerned with the past and present: forecasting for the future may be based on this. Yet the development of expert systems using computers may become commonplace in social work (Glastonbury, 1985; Toole and Winfield, 1986) and may improve our practice decisions. In the meantime, the referrals for today await our attention!

4

Crisis Intervention

In this chapter I explore what is meant by the word 'crisis', as it relates to a specific social work approach. Brief case examples are used to illuminate the distinction between crises and emergencies and offer as models practitioners who were able to 'stand still', that is remain calm, in the face of such situations. The stages of crisis resolution, the signs and symptoms to look for and the difference between stress and crisis are noted. Usually crisis intervention is associated with preventive work and this is given attention. A framework which summarises the main ideas of the approach is followed by a detailed look at techniques which may be used in the initial, continuing and closing phases of intervention.

What do we mean by 'crisis'?

The word 'crisis' is frequently misused by social workers. They use it in response to an emergency referral or to describe the fact that overworked agencies are engaged in the provision of minimal service. Thus I sometimes hear staff saying, 'We only have time to do crisis intervention.' This signifies a lack of understanding of the concepts and methods. This kind of inaccurate use of the term may have prevented a more thorough testing of the model so that we cannot yet dignify the crisis approach with the status of 'theory'. I hope that, having read this, the reader will avoid uncritical and undifferentiated use of the term so as correctly to understand and apply the ideas.

Nevertheless defining crisis *is* difficult (O'Hagan, 1986). Professional use of the term is hampered by the lay person's

38

portrayal of crisis as drama, panic, chaos – the 'economic crisis' and so on. The accepted definition for our purposes is that '*a crisis is an upset in a steady state*', (Rapoport, 1970, p. 276). The steady state is also called 'equilibrium' or 'homeostasis', referring to our usual 'healthy' level of coping with the many life problems which come our way: life is a problem-solving process and crises form a normal part of our development. In a crisis, our habitual strengths and mechanisms for coping do not work: we fail to adjust either because the situation is new to us, or it has not been anticipated or a series of events becomes overwhelming. Crises have a peak or sudden turning-point; as this peak approaches, tension mounts and energy for coping is mobilised; we 'rise to the occasion' (Parad and Caplan, 1965, p. 57).

If a person is overpowered by external, interpersonal or intrapsychic forces, (that is, conflicting needs) then homeostasis is lost for a time. Caplan (1964) postulates that this process lasts for about six weeks, during which period the individual strives to regain a sense of balance or harmony. (The same phenomenon can occur on a larger scale with organisations or whole communities who have experienced a disaster, such as the Bradford fire in England in 1985). During the disorganised, recovery stage, human beings are more receptive to being helped because they need to restore the predictability of their worlds and are therefore less defensive.

Sometimes crises can revive old, unresolved issues and these can add to the sense of being overburdened and overwhelmed, as the following two case examples demonstrate.

Case examples

1. Mrs Todd was admitted to an elderly persons' home following the death of her husband and at the request of her daughter who could no longer manage. Six months later Mrs Todd refused to get out of bed for a week saying that there was no point. Physical explanations were ruled out. Sensitive questioning by the residential social worker revealed that the

woman had never come to terms with the loss of her husband, nor had she subsequently acknowledged the sense of being abandoned by her family. The client's denial of her grief, plus the loss of control over solving her own problems had resulted in confused thinking and withdrawal.

2. The ward sister of the local hospital contacted the area social worker who had spent some months working intensively with the Smith family. They had carefully planned the return home of their daughter, who had become disabled following a road accident. Adaptations and equipment were installed in the home and community services organised. On being given a definite discharge date Mr Smith had become uncontrollably tearful, refusing to take his young child home, saying that he could not cope. In working through this period of crisis, the social worker helped Mr Smith to begin to 'think straight', to recognise his emotional outpourings as normal and to explore all the resources which would be made available. The overload effect of being confronted with the reality of discharge was later connected by the Smiths to their long-standing unhappy marriage, to which they had become resigned. Mr Smith's current despair therefore was uncoupled from his chronic disappointment at having 'failed' to find ways of achieving happiness in the marital relationship. Short term crisis intervention was, in this case, renegotiated so that longer help, using a more open-ended approach was offered.

Hudson (1982) complains that crisis intervention is preached more than it is practised. Neither of these referrals required a 'fire fighting' response and possibly may not have been given any priority since they were not the stuff of drama or danger. Yet the clients were in crisis; they perceived themselves as having no autonomy or mastery for coping. They needed immediate, calm support from a clear-headed worker. One such professional said to me recently, 'When I am dealing with a crisis, firstly I *stand still*.' This seems to be a wise precaution against any temptation to tear around, almost in crisis oneself.

To sum up, crises occur throughout life; we constantly make adaptive manoeuvres in order to cope and maintain our equilibrium. But if we meet a novel situation, experience too many life events, or become overloaded with old, unresolved conflicts, then a crisis occurs. This is a time limited process during which we become disorganised in thinking and be-having: mounting tension can result in the generation of mental energy for getting the problem solved. Crises can be perceived as a threat, a loss or a challenge encompassing danger but also opportunity for growth, especially when the situation is mastered and new methods of coping found or when there is a second chance to correct non-adjustment to an earlier event.

Stages of crisis resolution

The stages of crisis resolution are similar to the phases of grief work (C. R. Smith, 1983; Parkes, 1986). The steady state or equilibrium is lost when the crisis occurs; the person becomes disorganised; attempts to recover a predictable world tend to be of the 'two steps forward and one step back' variety; following attempts to deny the problem, there are efforts to recover in spite of it; reorganisation to the previous level of coping is then possible. Increased competence and growth could be the outcome, but if the person does not master theses stages there could be regression towards resignation, despair, breakdown, illness or other forms of maladjustment. According to Caplan (1964) *a crisis has four phases*:

1. There is a rise in tension in response to a stress or event. Habitual problem-solving mechanisms are called upon to preserve the steady state.
2. A further rise in tension and disorganisation occurs as the individual (or system) avoids doing anything or makes desperate attempts to cope.
3. Inner and outer resources are put into action and some kind of solution is reached, but this may be incomplete or lead to diminished problem solving in the future.
4. Beyond this, personality and behaviour can become so disorganised that a 'nervous breakdown' occurs; there could be magical thinking such as 'if I don't think about it the problem will disappear', retreat into fantasy and a loss of touch with reality.

The *signs* of someone in crisis may be difficult to spot, as we saw with Mrs Todd. However, since some of the responses follow a typical or predictable path this can give us some clues. So we know that in the period of distress, the person is striving to gain control and is open to suggestions which will aid recovery: phrases used may include 'I can't cope'; 'I feel a failure'; 'I don't know where to turn' or 'It is hopeless'. Often thoughts and behaviour are agitated, confused, hostile, ashamed or helpless. People may become withdrawn or irritable with their friends and relatives. Attempts to solve difficulties appear chaotic and unfocused. One client, unhappy in his new department at work, walked around all day muttering to himself; this could have been mistaken for a form of mental illness. Some physiological changes occur too so that bodily complaints such as sleeplessness, tension and so on are apparent.

Occasionally, the word 'stress' is used interchangeably with crisis, but the latter is short term and has more productive potential in terms of offering opportunity for improved functioning. Nevertheless there is a relationship between *life events and stress* and a great deal of research has gone into this (Schless *et al.*, 1977). Crises occur when making social readjustments which can be stressful: yet what constitutes a crisis for one person may not do so for another. This has been demonstrated with the responses given to the Social Readjustment Rating Scale (Holmes and Rahe, 1967). Here the psychological significance of ordinary occurrences like moving house or promotion caused widely differing reactions amongst the respondents who rated such items on the questionnaires. I have used something similar with groups of students, asking them to rate from 0 to 100 (low to high) their reactions to events such as starting a social work course, changing their incomes up or down and visiting relatives. The different order of magnitude and degrees of *meaning*, which are not universally held within the group, come as a surprise. I think it is necessary to underline this concept of meaning because therein lies, for me, the essence of crisis intervention – the focus for helping is what the event or stressor means to the individual: their perception, not one's own.

Preventive work and crisis intervention

There are two types of crisis, those which can be foreseen and those which are accidental. Amongst the former are all the life stage transitions such as moving into adolescence or middle age, which can be anticipated; the latter arc unforeseen circumstances such as illness or the loss of a job; they therefore carry less scope for offering preventive help. Because maturational or transitional crisis are actually expected evolutional changes for all of us, many larger social systems have started to plan and operate services to keep people healthy rather than simply react to cries for help on a case-by-case basis. Thus ante-natal clinics, drugs information in the media and teaching school children to say 'no' to strangers are all examples of preventive mental health: promoting well-being is seen to be preferable to 'picking up the pieces' later.

On a community level some enlightened planners have encouraged residents to play an active role in deciding where and how to be rehoused: when an area is being regenerated, a lack of consultation can lead to a lot of mental and physical distress, particularly when established neighbourhoods have been destroyed. Although Payne (1986) is sceptical about those with political and financial power devolving real decision making to local people, where this has been tried we have an example of *primary* prevention.

Secondary crisis prevention is offered by those agencies geared to helping after specific problems have arisen: examples of these are the women's aid refuges, suicide prevention centres, rape crisis services and organisations which help immigrants to adjust following the loss of their homeland (Marris, 1974). Both secondary and tertiary prevention (limiting the disabling effects of previous intervention and rehabilitation) is undertaken by psychiatric crisis intervention teams (Scott and Starr, 1981). These authors, believing that admission to a mental hospital removes the possibility of access to changing the context in which the symptoms arise, prefer to work with families and their networks whenever a 'plea for removal', (O'Hagan, 1986) is made. (Incidentally, a crisis admission to psychiatric care is more likely if the client is black, which is a disturbing finding by Rack, 1982.) Similarly, when you are asked to receive children into care or elderly people into homes, it is as well to investigate whether the request might be due to the fact that everyone involved is in crisis: simply rescuing any of the 'victims' by agreeing to care could block off an ideal opportunity to change the ways in which all members of the system interact (Byng-Hall and Bruggen, 1974; Byng-Hall and Campbell, 1981).

A framework for understanding crisis intervention

Before the specific techniques for helping are detailed, a summary of the crisis intervention approach is given below.

Theories and important concepts which contribute to the identification of crisis have developed as follows: (a) Psychoanalytic theories of personality, described in Chapter Six, where the ego directs energy for problem solving, appraises reality and helps us to cope, adapt and master conflicts. (b) Erikson (1965) building on this ego psychology, suggests that we grow through managing crisis points, which are stages in our development towards maturity. (c) Learning theorists made a contribution with ideas about cognitive insights, modelling coping behaviour for role transitions and repetitive rehearsal of effective problem solving (see Chapter Seven). (d) These contributions fuse with those from research studies into grief reactions (Lindemann, 1965) and the development of brief social work treatment (Reid and Shyne, 1969): time-limited work, as the chapter on task-centred work shows, can help to restore someone to their previous level of functioning; it also preserves autonomy and prevents dependence on the worker.

Problems for which this approach is relevant are maturational crisis such as leaving home and retirement, plus situational crises such as bereavement. People may perceive particular events as threatening to their life goals and may temporarily need support to surmount any distorted thinking and behaviour which get in the way of healthy adjustments.

Usually difficulties are current and pressing so that keeping a referral on a waiting-list would be inappropriate, as would taking a history, unless the present issue has reactivated an earlier sense of loss. Sometimes, crises are self-generated; clients may apparently live from one crisis to another and these situations are not relevant for this approach – longer-term support is usually necessary. (Examples of such lifestyles of chronic stress are graphically described by Mattinson and Sinclair in their book *Mate and Stalemate*, 1979.)

Goals are kept to a minimum, such as relief of symptoms, restoration to the previous level of coping, understanding what precipitated the condition, planning what the client can do to maintain maximum autonomy, and finding out what other resources could be used. If necessary, when current stresses have their origins in past life experiences, the goal might be to learn new ways of managing so as to ensure coping with future life events.

The client's role Occasionally, in crises, clients take unwise decisions or make inappropriate suggestions for solving the problem; with this method, the worker takes advantage of the client's willingness to trust and gives advice but ensures space to explore the crisis. By letting people 'tell the story to themselves,' they gain *cognitive awareness* of the stressful event and the balancing factors (such as social supports) which were assumed to be absent.

The worker's role At the beginning, middle and end of the process, the worker is using specific techniques. These are detailed below, with the major interventions italicised.

Techniques

In the first interview it is essential that the focus is kept on the present, asking 'What happened?', thereby *encouraging the client's cognitive grasp* of the situation. Comments such as 'You must feel awful' or 'No wonder you are upset' help to prompt the affective responses which block thinking. *Making an assessment* of the actual event and the causes which seem to have triggered it, plus the person's ego strengths, can be gleaned by questions such as 'When did things start to go wrong?'; 'How did you try to handle this?'; 'What happened then?'; 'What is happening now?' and 'Which supports can you call on?' Having gained some idea of the available and potential resources, the *worker outlines the next step*, that is, 'What is the most pressing problem?' The client is then asked to settle on one target area: 'So the most important thing is . . .?'

All the time, the social worker conveys hope and shows commitment to helping, cutting the overwhelming problem down into manageable bits. A *contract* for further work is spelled out in specific, concrete terms such as 'Let's concentrate on . . . You do . . . I'll do . . ..' Optimism is used to reduce the client's anxiety. The aim, at this early stage, is to start to *build a relationship* based, not on time, but on the worker's expertise and authenticity (this keeps the person in touch with reality).

As the client's thinking is clarified, it is necessary to *re-establish a sense of autonomy* by giving him/her something to do before the next meeting; equally, this can be achieved by letting the agreement about when and how frequently to meet be decided by the individual: a client self-demand schedule such as 'I think I need to see you four more times over the next two weeks; by then I should be in a better position to cope.'

Further contact In the middle phase, according to Golan (1978) the worker might concentrate on *obtaining missing data*, for example, 'Can you tell me more about . . .?' The emphasis is still on the here-and-now but there may be *links with past conflicts*. Pointing out possible connections helps to correct cognitive perception, keeps the problem in the foreground and therefore 'real': the helper has to be the '*voice of reality*', showing the difference between 'what is' and 'what ought to be'. For example, I recently interviewed a couple, both in their second marriages, who had hurt each other during a violent row. I had to unlock each partner's distorted view of the other by suggesting, 'Could you be confusing Ann's wish to have more of your time with your previous wife's over-reliance on you?' and to Ann, 'Could you be mixing up Joe's staying late at work with your ex-husband's neglect of you?' Tension is reduced by *ventilation*, letting the person talk.

Then help is given to sort out what worked and did not work in the problem-solving attempts; 'So you did . . . Did it work . . .?' Alternative ways of coping and overlooked resources can be explored to restore equilibrium and to *develop a future pattern* for using such help. By working out specific tasks together, aiming for achievable goals, the social worker acts as a model for competent problem solving: by *setting homework*; 'Before we next meet, I'd like you to think how you could . . .' the stage is set for encouraging change in thinking and behaving so that the client can continue to cope.

The termination phase of crisis intervention, possibly the last two interviews, should have been built into the beginning agreement. Once the crisis is resolved and homeostasis restored, it would be harmful to prolong active intervention of this kind as it could ignore natural growth potential. Reminding the client how much time there is left, *reviewing progress and planning for the future* prevent dependency. Premature termination by the client: 'I can cope now, so I don't want to see you any more' may be a 'flight into health' about which Rapoport (1970) gives guidance – ending contact with someone needs accurate assessment to prevent the person from failing to manage yet again in the future, thereby rendering themselves even more vulnerable to life's other problems (L. L. Smith, 1979).

In conclusion, when you are working in crisis situations you need to be active, directive, authentic, give advice and take advantage of people's readiness to trust you: when energy is being used in the struggle to regain the steady state, defense mechanisms are lowered. The setting of time limits, for example, four to six interviews encourages the efforts towards change and prevents regression. Once the acute stage is successfully negotiated, there is scope to renegotiate contact in order to work on longer-term problems, if necessary. Although cognitive restructuring may have taken place, in that present difficulties have been uncoupled from earlier ones, the aim of this approach is not self-understanding as such: rather the goals are for the client to think clearly about problems and learn how to split them into manageable pieces. Relationships depend not on long term involvement, but on your authority and professional skills, plus your ability to 'stand still' that is, keep calm when confronted with people or systems in crisis.

5

Task-Centred Work

In this chapter I will concentrate on how task-centred practice has been developed, examining some of the latest research into its effectiveness and analysing how it compares with crisis intervention. A framework for understanding the main ideas will be outlined and case examples used to illustrate the methods in action.

How the task-centred approach developed

It seems hard to believe, in this era of intake teams, brief intervention and goal-orientated work that, prior to the 1970s, much casework was undertaken on a long-term basis. Perlman, in 1957, took a forward step by formulating social work as a problem-solving process. But traditionally, particularly in America, a favoured method of work involved passive exploration of clients' feelings and trying to analyse underlying personality difficulties. There was a tendency to talk about, rather than take action on problems. Also, some clients received help for years and compulsive care giving by helpers frequently resulted in the difficulties becoming the responsibility and 'property' of the worker (Buckle, 1981).

In my early days as a mental welfare officer, I kept cases open for years, visiting on a friendly but aimless basis. My interviews were diffuse and somewhat unplanned. If I did have goals they were Utopian ones of 'cure'; these 'goals in mind' stayed where they were and were rarely shared with anyone: occasionally, I worked alongside clients on the needs which they had specified, but, essentially, I was what Davies (1985) calls a 'maintenance mechanic'. He argues that this is a

49

key social work role and suggests that craving for change is textbook idealism.

Some practitioners in the 1970s were not content with a lack of concern for effectiveness (Fischer, 1976). Yet many criticisms may have been unjustified in that the reasons why some interventions failed to show any demonstrable effects might have been due in part to the vagueness of the workers' goals and evaluators trying to measure the immeasurable, such as 'happiness'. But, researchers contended, there was a need to study the treatment process and its relation to change.

In America, in 1969, a four-year study into brief and extended casework was published (Reid and Shyne, 1969). Clients with family problems were offered two contrasting patterns of social work intervention: one was an experimental brief service of Planned Short Term Treatment, (P.S.T.T.) consisting of eight interviews; the other was the usual practice in the agency of long-term service lasting up to eighteen months. To everyone's surprise, the clients in the short-term group improved more than those given the continued service. In fact the later tended to deteriorate! The authors hypothesised that a law of diminishing returns was operating. Once help is extended beyond a certain point, clients may lose confidence in their own ability to cope and become dependent on the worker. Also, when there is improvement, this will occur early on in treatment regardless of the worker having long-term goals. This research was taken up in Britain by researchers at the National Institute for Social Work (Goldberg *et al.*, 1985). They quote similar findings from a study into the probation service: reconviction rates in one-year probation orders were lower than expected and, in three-years orders, higher than expected. (We will return to this series of research projects later in the chapter.)

The vital elements in Reid and Shyne's experiment seemed to be that brief periods of service, concentrating on limited goals chosen by the client, were often more effective and more durable than open-ended work. It appeared that setting a time-limit led to the expectation that rapid change would occur, thus increasing the energy and motivation of all the participants. The social workers in the project concentrated on advice giving and active exploration of problems and aimed for unambitious, specific goals. Their performance was committed and hopeful: there might have been placebo effects adding to the success; consumer satisfaction studies always mention these qualities as beneficial ones, alongside speedy and comprehensible intervention (Sainsbury, 1986).

The first book describing 'task-centred practice' as such was published in 1972 (Reid and Epstein) giving the results of the tests into the elements which seemed responsible for the success of the approach. An even more systematic and goal-directed framework had been developed which suggested that there should be a maximum of twelve interviews within three months, focusing on limited, achievable goals which were *chosen by the client*. Practitioners who tried out the ideas helped to further refine the model (Reid and Epstein, 1977) Today, task-centred practice deals with *eight problem areas* which cover most of the referrals met by social workers. They are:

Interpersonal conflict
Dissatisfaction in Social Relations
Problems with Formal Organisations
Difficulties in Role Performance
Problems of Social Transition
Reactive Emotional Distress
Inadequate Resources
Behavioural Problems
(Reid, 1978; Reid and Hanrahan, 1981).

There are definite steps to be taken in the process: *five phases* in helping clients to achieve their own modest goals.

1. *Problem Exploration* when clients' concerns are elicited, clarified, defined in explicit, behavioural terms and ranked in order of importance to the client.

2. *Agreement* is reached with the client on the target for change, which is then classified by the worker under the previous eight categories.

3. *Formulating an Objective* which has been decided jointly; agreement is reached on the frequency and duration of the contract (NB: a written contract may be alien to some social classes or ethnic groups.)

4. *Achieving the Task(s)*, for which no prescribed methods or techniques are proposed.

5. *Termination* is built in from the beginning; when reviewing the achievements, the worker's efforts are examined alongside those of the clients.

Throughout the development of this approach in America, similar research was being conducted in this country by Matilda Goldberg and her colleagues (Goldberg *et al*., 1977). They found that the model, used by a Social Services team in Buckinghamshire England applied only to a minority of clients. Those with a need for practical resources, who acknowledged that they had a problem, fared best: involuntary clients or those who had chronic, complex problems were less amenable.

Nevertheless there were *positive gains for the workers* in the project who improved their capacity for clearer thinking and forward planning. Tackling small, manageable objectives, rather than vague, global ones, proved more realistic: social workers felt less guilty about being unable to sort out everything. As a result three experimental projects using task-centred work were set up in a probation setting, with two intake teams and a hospital social work department (Goldberg *et al*., 1985). As the findings and conclusions hold for all three settings and client groups they are worth summarising; they also give us an up-to-date and rounded picture of the approach.

The model proved applicable to between a half and two-thirds of all cases. The remaining groups largely ended the attempt to be task-centred after the problem search resulted in no agreed target problem. Most clients who completed the contract were pleased with the methods and said that their problems were reduced. Other clients who could not be helped included those with endless emergencies, with deep-seated, lifelong difficulties. The skills required of the workers included an ability to listen and grasp what the client was bothered about; to know when to use systematic communication and when to be responsive (this is described below); to have the ability to renegotiate the conditions for giving and accepting help; to learn to act as a partner, not just a provider; to be explicit about time-limits and to remind the client about ending the contract, without harping on this. Difficulties were encountered by the workers who saw that it was over ambitious to treat clients as equals when they have no control over resources. Additionally, when people were under surveillance as part of statutory duties, they actually had very little power in terms of being partners. These remain as unresolved issues, but at least they remind us how paternalistic some of our arrangements really are.

The difficulties I have with the approach, and these are echoed by many students, are mainly to do with the technique of using two communication styles. It is specified in task-centred practice that the worker use *systematic and responsive communications*. If I analyse what these terms mean, it will emerge that this is something of a paradox. Systematic communications are those which concentrate on the step by step way of problem-solving, of keeping the client to the agreed task in hand, so as to reach the target problem. Generally, the worker's responses should logically follow themes which stop the change effort becoming diffuse. Sometimes a client may discuss difficulties which are not part of the agreed focus. So, for example, if I have a client who has agreed that the problem tasks are to focus on controlling children's behaviour, I will be in a quandary if marital difficulties continue to crop up. The uncertainty will arise because I will be unsure if I need to acknowledge the marital disharmony in order to help the client accomplish our agreed treatment steps. It is difficult to know when communication is becoming unsystematic. There is also always the possibility that we have chosen our focus unwisely or that it is no longer a valid goal to work towards. Of course, in practice, it is permissible to allow some discussion and then, in view of the limited time available, bring the client back to the task. Or I might say, 'We often seem to drift towards talking about your marriage. Do we need to rethink what we are aiming for?' Excessive clinging to the contract would be robot-like and would not fulfil the second communication requirement of being responsive.

Responsive communications express interest in the client's messages and recognise their value. The worker conveys empathic understanding, showing that what the problem means to the other person is understood. Attention is given too to building upon the client's own communications and not introducing ideas which are only of interest to the worker. The Rogerian view of empathic understanding, which we witnessed in Chapter Three, depended on conveying this verbally and non-verbally. This quality has to be combined with a structured use of time, which could face the helper with the dilemma, 'Can I be sensitive and business like?' In reality it is not necessary to lose an appreciation of the client's world in order to accomplish the step in hand. There are ways of communicating which preserve both qualities. It is possible to convey an understanding of the many other difficulties a person has while insisting that the task be returned to. If the client has agreed to a certain plan of work, then this will not be interpreted as a lack of interest. I have found too that it is seen as very responsive to enquire further into a passing remark, rather than to let it pass or change the subject. Whereas a non-directive counsellor might refrain from adding anything to a client's communication and just reflect it back, a responsive interviewer might stay within the other's frame of reference but ask questions which fill out the frame. So, for instance, if a client says, 'I'm confused', this is an incomplete sentence which could hide many meanings which it is important to bring to the surface by asking, 'About what?' Sometimes people delete, distort or generalise about their experiences: a responsive helper would never let a remark such as 'Nobody cares' pass – it would be essential to ask, 'Who specifically does not care?'

The other limitations which have been found with the method are the expectations which other agencies and referrers have about the role of social workers 'who will always be around'. Medical practitioners, school personnel, social security officials and other members of the community have to be weaned away from the belief that once referred we will look after people and visit for ever. Everyone has to be re-educated to the ideas behind task-centred work.

The benefits of using task-centred methods

Before I go on to discuss when task-centred ideas might be used and how this approach compares with crisis intervention, I wish to summarise the main benefits. Incidentally, though, just as we saw the term 'crisis intervention' being used loosely, so too is there misunderstanding of the words 'task-centred'. It does not mean 'doing tasks', or the worker adopting a problem-solving approach to a workload. It has a specific definition as a method of social work in which clients are helped to carry out problem-alleviating tasks within agreed periods of time. The important difference is that the client is the change agent, helping the worker to assess and choose what the priorities for change ought to be and then agreeing the necessary goals and tasks.

Task-centred practice fits well into intake teams, which were set up to handle short-term work and protect the clients on long-term caseloads (Buckle, 1981). Any practice which ensures that there is no misunderstanding about why contact is taking place is likely to be more successful and more honest. A clear acknowledgement that the worker is an agent of social control or a needed therapist may sort out some of the ambiguity for client and worker. Forward planning on cases is improved, respect for the client is built in, social work is demystified, goals become modest rather than encouraging a 'happy ending' syndrome, termination is openly planned rather than tailing off and clients become proud of their achievements.

The task-centred approach is the one most favoured by those who are trying to devise models for ethnic-sensitive practice (Devore and Schlesinger, 1981). This is because the methods do not further oppress people by taking over their lives or implying the worker's knowing better than they do what the problems entail. It takes into account the person's own view of the problem and ideas for change. There is no mystery about what the worker is doing and because she/he is as accountable as the client in carrying out agreed tasks, this helps to lessen the sense of powerlessness when faced with 'authority' figures. Apart from the rigid time-limits, which ignore the ethnic perspective, task-centred work is beneficial in that it:

1. Takes into account individual and collective experiences during the stages of problem exploration, agreement and

formulating objectives. The source of the problem does not necessarily reside 'in' the person: more attention is paid to external systems where the scope for advocacy is recognised. Unlike other therapies which may unknowingly overstress the negative effects of discrimination and disadvantage, when the client's view of the problem is what matters, there is scope to see the beneficial effects of black or racial membership, cohesion, 'peoplehood' and identity.

2. Does not rely on self-disclosure or a one-way helping relationship. Self-realisation is not emphasised and there is a tendency to deal with what is in the present. Requests for concrete help are respected without looking for underlying difficulties, and yet should help be needed with emotional problems, these can be re-negotiated openly between worker and client when trust has been established.

Rather than look for 'suitable cases', you could apply this method to all your workload. Referrals may get no further than the first two stages of the problem exploration and categorisation within the eight-problem typology; in this instance you would have *task-centred assessments*; clients may choose to go no further or else to be helped using another of the approaches discussed in this book. Similarly, you might apply the ideas to work with couples, families and groups. Atherton (1982) using partially and fully task-centred approaches, as above, believes that the methods have drama- tically altered her ways of working, both with clients and in her role as a team leader/staff supervisor. She says that she can relax at each interview, knowing what are the problems, tasks and goals and helping the client or worker to find creative solutions.

Some practitioners comment that this model is akin to crisis intervention (Gibbons *et al.*, 1979). Both encompass brief, focal work (Hutten, 1975/6). They are used when clients are temporarily unable to sort out their difficulties; the under- lying theory is that acute breakdown in problem coping triggers off corrective change forces. Additionally, time itself is used as a vehicle for change.

However, in task-centred practice, clients are expected clearly to conceptualise problems and solutions, to have an equal partnership with the worker, to engage in energetic problem-solving activity and to be able to stick to the contract; whilst significant difficulties may be tackled, these need not be crises in the accepted sense. Also there is an assumption that clients can maintain focus long enough to carry out the plan, independently if need be. The work is highly structured and discussions rarely wander from the task in hand; the goals are usually behaviourally specified and the whole programme tightly scheduled. As has been seen, there may be turbulent changes occurring in crisis which require a more flexible, responsive, worker-directed pattern, where the goals are primarily cognitive mastery of an overwhelming situation. Clients in crisis are unlikely to be able to cope with the demands of task-centred work.

Case examples

Mr Taylor was a fifty-seven-year-old widower who had spent his working life as a ship's captain. Travelling around the world had left him with no friends in his locality and his married son, who lived many miles away, could only visit him two or three times a year. Following a stroke six months previously, the client had 'vegetated' in a day centre for physically handicapped people. Rehabilitation efforts had ceased: staff complained that Mr Taylor was uncooperative and aggressive; they even wondered if he was depressed, as he slumped all day in a wheelchair, keeping himself to himself.

The social worker received a referral from the care staff to sort out the numerous debts which had accrued because the client had not claimed any benefits. She found that Mr Taylor, far from being hostile, was a gentle, shy man who was not used to discussing his private affairs. When he heard about the task-centred ideas, which would not pry into his background, he was pleased to talk about his problems. He defined these as 'problems with formal organisations' and 'inadequate resources'. The contract was agreed that they would meet weekly to work on two target problems:

1. To pay off rent, telephone and fuel bills within the following three months.

2. To claim outstanding benefits from social security, insurance companies and salary from previous employers.

General tasks, such as writing letters, listing the debts, making phone calls and deciding who would do what were dealt with in the first two meetings. A schedule was drawn up about the frequency and duration of the meetings and letting the centre staff know what they would be doing.

Every Monday at the same time the social worker wheeled Mr Taylor to a pleasant spot where they discussed how the debts could be cleared and which were the most pressing. Responsibilities were allocated and each week they reviewed each other's task accomplishments. Sometimes the worker had to obtain some necessary forms and give the client instructions on how to complete them, but no revision of the contract was needed. The client not only cleared his debts and claimed his allowances, but also began to talk about his past and his *future*: something he seemed to have forgotten about.

Mr Taylor confided to the worker his fears about living alone and not knowing anyone around him, even the other people in the centre. They re-negotiated a further contract whereby:

1. He would start a conversation with one of his companions at lunch every day.
2. He would write to his son telling him how he had sorted out his finances, and ask if he could visit him some time.

Because the client's manner was so approachable, physiotherapy and occupational therapy were restarted, resulting in an ability to walk with a tripod. The son made a visit and offered his father a home. The staff marvelled at the change, for which neither Mr Taylor nor his social worker were given any credit!

The second situation was met by a student on a four-month community work placement: he was asked to make an assessment of the needs felt by the residents in one street which had achieved notoriety due to their 'criminal and irresponsible' behaviour. Intervention by police, Social Services, Social Security and housing officials seemed to have exacerbated the stigmatising and labelling of the tenants. Their council houses were almost derelict: empty homes were, in fact, devoid of roofs and floorboards (stolen, it was alleged, by the remaining neighbours).

Having completed a community profile (Glampson *et al.*, 1975) the student started to make contact with the residents by knocking on their doors with a survey which asked them what they would like to see changed in the street. Perhaps not surprisingly, the majority of people wanted the professionals 'off their backs'; there were complaints that being viewed as 'undesirable' and trying to 'dump all and sundry' on their doorsteps was greatly resented; additionally, there was no way of leaving and being rehoused due to this 'bad press'.

One tenant had several daughters and their children living in the street; she had been an asset to a former community worker's efforts to establish summer play schemes. She was angry at the Housing Department in particular, believing that they were giving the place a bad name: her goal was to arrange a meeting to confront them about their housing policies.

Although this was not a fully task-centred project, in that the student did not have the time to agree on the other target problems by the residents, he did assist in getting a person of authority from the Housing Department to meet most of the tenants. Their concerns at being labelled were heard sympathetically: their ability to talk as a group was the beginning of a change of attitude on the part of the authorities. Now, some years later, the area has been refurbished as part of a larger, long-term project agreed between the private and the public sector.

To conclude, the main concepts and activities within this approach are summarised below by means of a framework for understanding task-centred practice.

A framework for understanding task-centred work

Theories which underly the task-centred approach are really only concepts. They include the crisis notion that focused help given at the right time is as effective as long-term service.

This is because temporary breakdowns in coping with problems set in motion forces for change; these forces are mainly clients' motivation to reduce problems to a manageable level. Another concept is that the imposition of time-limits speeds up change by implying that the problem can be solved in the time allowed: this enhances motivation. By concentrating energy on limited, achievable goals, it is likely that success will breed success. The goals are, as far as possible, specified in concrete behavioural terms. Thus a global goal, 'to improve the marital relationship' would be replaced by 'I will show my wife that I care for her by taking her out each week.' The client is seen, not as a victim of inner drives or external constraints, but as an autonomous, problem-solving change agent. No specific problem-orientated theory exists at this point which would help us to understand how people conceptualise and deal with their difficulties. But the philosophy upon which this approach depends is that we help people to do what they want, so that motivation is guided and strengthened.

Problems are psychosocial in nature and comprise eight categories which describe problem situations rather than client types. The problems selected for attention by the client and worker should be feasible ones. They should be prioritised by the client. In order that change be likely, necessary skills and resources, or the opportunity to create them, should exist.

Goals are modest, achievable, specific and often framed in behavioural terms; they are the ones chosen by the client as the most important (rather than what the worker thinks might be 'good' for someone.)

The client's role is to pursue desirable and feasible tasks. Often there may be multiple tasks and sub-tasks to be detailed in an agreement with the worker. There should be adequate capacity for self-determination so that the plan of action can be adhered to.

Worker's role is to make explicit the time-limits and to assist in the problem search, target and tasks. The worker gives encouragement and information and, if necessary, offers direction and explanations.

Techniques and activities include *problem specification*

such as, 'When you try to get your son to go to school, what does he do; who helps you; how do you react; what happens then . . .?'; *task planning* includes generating alternatives, task agreement, planning the details of implementation and summarising; for example, 'So, what else could you try . . .'? could you do this before we meet next time . . .? you will ask your husband to back you up . . . so we have agreed that . . .; *analysing obstacles*; *using simulation*, (role-play, rehearsal, modelling); *planning practitioner tasks*, such as letter writing; *structuring interview time*; *planning* 'who will do what' and *reviewing*.

6

The Psychosocial Approach

In this chapter I will explore the psychosocial approach and examine some of the criticisms of it. I will consider its relevance and show how we use some of the ideas all the time, particularly in trying to understand people and support them. I will draw a framework of the main principles which underly the approach and illustrate parts of the treatment processes by means of a case example.

The psychosocial approach as a method of understanding

If you have ever been puzzled by irrational behaviour, your own or anyone else's, insights from psychoanalysis could help. By drawing on some features of psychoanalysis, the psychosocial approach has offered us the chance to understand feelings, motives and behaviour which would otherwise be far from self-evident. Some social workers working in special hospitals with dangerous clients have to have a very deep understanding of why some people's personalities are so disordered that they cannot control aggressive or sexual urges. But all social workers, working with any type of client, need to be able to make sense out of what might be viewed by lay people as nonsense. People have inner worlds and outer realities. Practice which takes only the latter into account may continually be off target. Everyone, and that includes us, has vulnerabilities; we do not always know why we do certain things, why we are attracted to some clients and not others and so forth. Thus, there is no 'us and them'; in this respect we are the same as those we help.

The psychosocial approach is essentially a method of

62

understanding the person as well as the problem. Certain procedures or techniques are involved and these are detailed later. The model is usually linked to the work of Hollis (1964) but the origins of the approach can be traced to the then radical ideas of Mary Richmond, (1922): she believed that a 'social diagnosis' should be formulated prior to giving help which would involve indirect treatment, (environmental manipulation) and/or direct treatment, (influencing the way people think, feel and behave). This became known as the Diagnostic School of social work. Later, Freudian psychoanalytic insights, particularly personality theory, began to feed into these views in order that individualised forms of helping could be offered. This is why the term 'differential treatment approach' was used, subsequently known as psychodynamic casework or the psychosocial approach. The aim was to study, diagnose and treat the person-in-situation, that is, the psychosocial whole.

There has been a great deal of emotional and perhaps ill-informed debate about this method of social work, which will be addressed later. But antagonism may have been justified because the processes seemed to dwell overmuch on study and diagnosis at the expense of actually doing anything. Additionally, there was a tendency for some caseworkers to neglect the social element in their work, blaming the problem on an individual's personality, which could be too readily categorised as 'neurotic', 'manipulative', 'narcissistic' or whatever else came to mind.

Today we may have swung too much the other way, since agencies can move into action without a thorough attempt to understand the *person* with the problem. Indeed some students strongly resist any attempts to get to know their clients beyond giving welfare benefits advice and straightforward provision of services. They see intimacy as intrusion and interference, which of course it is if there is no purpose in mind. On closer inspection though, those in training admit that often the resistance to getting involved lies in their own fear of doing so. They worry about getting *too* involved, taking home their clients' problems; there is concern that people get damaged if we look beyond the surface and deal with emotional difficulties; frequently helpers do not know themselves nor their own strengths and weaknesses and in protecting clients may be protecting themselves.

In Chapter Two I cautioned against always asking the client why they felt, thought or acted in certain ways (usually they do not know). However in this approach it would be valid for the worker to ponder, 'Why does this person do such and such?' Equally some clients want to know, 'Why am I like this?' and, when appropriate, self-understanding is one of the goals of psychosocial intervention. Accurate plans for the future may depend on this. Also, for some people, the past is still part of their present and this can have an effect on future goal planning.

By failing to understand the person as well as the problem, we are liable to waste time, dismiss clients as being beyond help, become impatient with them and continually miss the point. I once ineffectively spent two years helping a woman with a rehousing problem, becoming intolerant when numerous house moves produced no change. Her needs were far more fundamental, being tied up largely with her incapacity for being alone (see Winnicott, 1957).

More recently other analysts besides Freud have contributed to the theoretical base of this model, notably Erikson (1965). His personality theory highlights the way in which we are affected by interpersonal, organisational and societal factors, as well as intrapsychic forces. Both his theories and Freud's contributions stress ego functioning that is, how people adapt and solve problems. The concepts from ego psychology are central to the psychosocial approach and are accordingly summarised here, drawing principally from the work of these two theorists.

Assessing a person's ego strengths

Freud conceptualised the personality system as a dynamic set of interacting forces designated as id, ego and super-ego. The impulses originating from the id are governed by the pleasure principle whilst the super-ego prohibits these chaotic drives. The ego, in order to avoid the pain of inner conflict and outer dangers, thinks of consequences anticipates events and works out solutions: it helps us to face three ways, to 'stop, look and listen' (Garrett, 1958). Thus the primary function of the ego is to balance inner needs and outer reality. An assessment of ego strengths is needed as a guide to offering appropriate intervention.

When talking about ego strengths, we are not referring to a fixed condition but to a dynamic, ever-changing capacity to cope with frustration, control impulses, make mature relationships and use defence mechanisms appropriately. Denial, displacement and projection are some of these mechanisms which help people to cope with conscious and unconscious anxiety. An individual's age, intellect and the intensity of pressures all affect ego functioning. Even if the problem lies outside the person, ego strengths need to be assessed because motivation or a reluctance to work on a situation will be influenced by the balance of hope and discomfort felt by the person. The height of maturity is when we gain the unusual ego strength of giving ourselves approval, rather than doing things to gain the good opinion of others. Most of us and our clients will probably never gain this level of self-actualisation; our purpose in trying to gauge the level of ego development is so that we can plan how much responsibility the client can take for managing problems and how much support we need to give. For instance, it would be necessary to confirm that a person has adequate capacity for tolerating self-scrutiny before any attempt was made to promote insight.

Freud's psychoanalytic theory of personality development, the oral, anal, phallic and latency periods (see Jacobs, 1986) largely equates with Erikson's (1965) 'Eight Stages of Man' which are more readily understood and applied by social workers. He suggests that human beings develop a sense of self through interpersonal relationships and mastering the adjustments and crises of life transitions: his progressive model shows how we might or might not develop an ego capacity for trust, self-control, purpose, competence, identity, intimacy, productivity and wisdom.

When helping adults who appear to have 'infantile' needs or whose behaviour is baffling, it is useful to assess at what stage of development they could be stuck, especially if this is connected with a past trauma: the concept of regression suggests that when people break down due to internal or external pressure, the collapse usually goes back as far as the stage at which these issues were not satisfactorily resolved. Thus we see, in direct work with children, that what might be called 'watershed therapies' can help them to regress, revisit painful feelings and build ego strengths undeveloped in the past. At the same time, those clients who seem unable to manage their lives (Kaufman, 1966) are equally in need of restitutive parent–child experiences, which the social worker may be able to give. These are the adults who antagonise agencies because of their neediness and their inability to care for anyone else.

For example, there is the mother who forgets to have food in the house for her baby because her own childlike needs are dominant, or the client who uses the money we obtain for the gas bill to buy cigarettes. Some people are so emotionally stressed by even a small matter, like keeping an appointment, that we have to be prepared to do a great deal of nurturing. We often have to give material things, because verbal communication may have little meaning. Their lives may have been marked by inconsistency, desertion, a feeling that no one cares or the intrusion of many authority figures; we have to provide consistency and a relationship which shows that we care in obvious ways.

Before moving on to how psychosocial methods have been criticised, I want to emphasise again that ego strengths must be assessed before attempting any self-awareness programme with clients. Indiscriminate 'laying bare' can lead to a personality becoming overwhelmed, either through super-ego, instinctual impulses or environmental stresses. For instance, the immature ego of the child or that of the psychotic needs help in maintaining resistance; interpretation of inner feelings would not be attempted (Prins, 1975).

Criticisms of the psychosocial approach

In Britain, the psychosocial approach has been a controversial aspect of social work thought and practice for many years. In 1959, Barbara Wootton's *Social Science and Social Pathol-*

ogy attacked social caseworkers for posing as miniature psychoanalysts. Wootton declared that, rather than search for underlying reasons for behaviour, the social worker would do better to 'look superficially on top', especially if help was sought with practical difficulties.

Nowadays there appears to be a great deal of 'looking superficially on top'. Maybe social workers do not feel equipped to do more than this: certainly according to James and Wilson (1986) there is anxiety and hesitation in handling underlying 'marital' problems. Most busy social services departments may see their major role as providing advice and practical services (Finnister, 1986). I have argued, though, that even when the goal is service provision, it is beneficial to understand the psychosocial person-in-situation, so that resources are not wasted.

The psychosocial approach was so unmercifully denounced that, at one time, it was dropped from the syllabus in my own School of Social Work. There seemed to be a variety of explanations for this. One reason might have been the clinical and obscure jargon found in early casework literature; (students found phrases such as 'person-in-situation configuration' vague and pretentious! (Hollis, 1964). Also research found that clients were angry and resentful when workers, unable to offer money, refocused their efforts towards underlying emotional problems: some helpers recorded client dissatisfaction as their displaying 'negative transference'! (Mayer and Timms, 1970).

When behavioural approaches began to be taught on training courses the results of intervention with specific, overt actions could be seen and tested for effectiveness. Comparisons between the speed of change using psychosocial support versus behavioural techniques highlighted the utility of the latter (Hudson, 1975). Furthermore there was understandable objection to the classification of people using psychiatric terminology, such as 'paranoid personality'. Additionally, notions of a therapeutic relationship, self-disclosure, individualisation and the assumed 'pathological' effects of belonging to certain racial groups were especially criticised by ethnic-sensitive practitioners. There was criticism from what was then known as the 'radical social work school' that middle-class caseworkers concentrated too much on intra-psychic forces and 'insight giving', while overlooking the effects of organisational and structural deficiencies (Bailey and Brake, 1975). Freud's theories were seen to be divorced from the material world which shapes 'man's' consciousness, and were viewed as products of a capitalist society (Corrigan and Leonard, 1978). For some years it was unfashionable to be concerned about individuals, their feelings and the micro world of self-knowledge, autonomy and growth. Even today the psychosocial school is thought to aim for the adjustment of clients to our given environment (Jordan, 1987).

Behind this censure may have been the assumption that caseworkers were conservative (implying the opposite stereotype that community workers were radical. It is to be hoped that we can now appreciate that the reverse is just as likely to be the case.) It seems to me that we should avoid any either/or, good/bad, black/white arguments about the personal and political dimensions of practice. They are false divisions and foolishly ignore the interaction between private and public worlds. In fact Yelloly (1980) wondered if these distinctions prevented insight into the way personal consciousness is moulded by economic and political relations – an analysis undertaken by few authors (see Fromm, 1962). To illustrate this point, Yelloly uses the example of the women's movement showing how personal predicaments reflect political reality: she argues that psychoanalytic thought is not a repressive ideological instrument but a route to liberation, a way of gaining insight into the social and psychological chains which keep human beings captive.

The same point is made by feminist psychoanalysts. Thus, while some workers may criticise the psychosocial approach because of its dependence on Freudian psychoanalytic theory, which perpetuates the concept of the inferior power of women (Burden and Gottlieb, 1987), Freud's distinction between the sexes, conversely, is recognised by Mitchell (1984) as the key to understanding women's psychology and their oppression under patriarchy.

The relevance and utility of the psychosocial approach

Practitioners may be surprised to find that they use some of the psychosocial methods all the time. The goal is to modify the person, the situation or both by using two main procedures – *sustaining and modifying*; the more familiar are the *sustaining techniques*, namely ventilation (unburdening); realistic reassurance (ego strengthening); acceptance (super-ego softening); logical discussion (appraising a client's ability to reason and tolerate reality); demonstrating behaviour (the social worker offering the strength of his/her own ego); giving information (increasing motivation for problem solving); advice and guidance (a person initially identifying with a helper's views prior to acquiring self-management) and direct intervention (by enriching the environment or eliminating external stress, mental energy is released for productive work). These are the techniques we are using when we talk about 'support' or 'offering a relationship'.

Modifying procedures aim to reduce outer stress and increase ego awareness of previously unrecognised aspects of personality dynamics, (providing that the diagnosis of ego strengths has confirmed that self-scrutiny can be tolerated). Confrontation techniques include pointing out patterns of thinking, feeling and doing, and how clients may respond in stereotyped ways in relationships with others; for example, within the client/worker relationship itself. Clarification includes interpretations of the way a person's responses may be connected with the use of defences or the manner in which the past is inappropriately influencing the present. The task is to link incidents and feelings from 'then and now'; inner and outer reality are connected and then objective and subjective experience separated. The helper also initiates a joining of intellectual awareness and feelings; an example of this, with someone who suffers from irrational guilt, would be to offer a non-judgemental relationship – a 'corrective emotional experience': this reduces conflict between the id and the ego, releasing energy for adaptation and coping. Similarly, rational thinking can be restored by simply putting feelings into words, thereby enhancing intellectual control. Malan (1982) summarises the procedures as observations which link a person's use of defences to the anxiety connected to hidden feelings, usually originating in the past.

According to Jacobs (1986) psychodynamic approaches link what clients bring to us from 'out there', (their lives), 'in here', (the relationship with the helper) and 'back there', (the past). This forms a 'triangle of conflict' where the person struggles with the anxiety associated with current feelings, here-and-now feelings and those connected with the distant past (Malan, 1982). An example of this would be, 'You say that you get anxious with women in authority. I remember you said that your mother was the boss at home. I wonder if you are feeling worried because I am a woman who seems to be telling you what to do?' While there is some doubt about the effectiveness of this kind of interpretation, much so-called 'insight giving' in social work is often no more than offering a reflective discussion in order to clarify the question 'why?' with those clients who wish to understand themselves better.

Some social workers believe that we have borrowed from psychoanalysis ways of fundamentally restructuring personalities. Of course we are not qualified to do this; we have neither the authority nor the time and clients do not usually see this as our function. Hollis (1970) suggests that personality change has occurred to a small extent if a person merely sees problems differently, has more control over problems, improves decision-making, increases self-assertion or appreciates another point of view. So-called 'archeological digging' into the past is not necessary and radical personality change is not the goal of this method as the subsequent research into worker techniques revealed.

In the study insight-oriented workers very rarely attempted deep exploration of clients' personalities; instead they explored conscious and occasionally pre-conscious material (Reid, 1967). Reid found that no psychoanalytic techniques, such as the analysis of transference and resistance, free association or elucidation of unconscious motives, were ever used. The social workers preferred responses which stimulated clients to think about their motives, feelings and behaviour, in respect of specific social and interpersonal problems. The techniques which were aimed at modifying the person were interpretations such as 'You resent being used as a servant, but you always give in.' Some probing methods were used such as 'What do you think might lie behind your need to give in?' Some workers tentatively pointed out consequences: 'Do you think you invite being put upon by appearing willing to give in to others?' Even behavioural therapists (and some of my friends!) would not be shy about asking such questions. They hardly represent in-depth analysis.

In truth much of the 'bread and butter' of social work needs to acknowledge a debt to the insights of the psychoanalytic school. Preventive and rehabilitative programmes use ideas from separation and attachment (Bowlby, 1982); the long term psychological effects of child abuse (Finkelhor, 1984); the way people respond to being bereaved (Pincus, 1975) and the way children, and later adults, see themselves and their relationships as good or bad in 'object relations' terms (Wittenberg, 1970). The procedures have been shown to be relevant when working with individuals, families, groups and communities (Turner, 1978). After all, social situations and systems, such as political groups, are made up of interacting individuals whose psychological make-up might affect any plans made.

There are times in our work when we are faced with *puzzling events*. A young boy became hysterical when his male counsellor winked at him when they were having a meal. It transpired that this had reminded the boy about early sexual abuse from his swimming instructor. We may also need to explain to others, as well as ourselves, what behaviour may mean. Olive Stevenson wrote a very useful article about this some time ago (1963). She described how she had adapted her understanding and skills from psychoanalysis to various situations which could otherwise have defeated understanding.

Jennifer, aged ten, had been fostered since she was eighteen months old, having suffered many upheavals in her first year of life. She had spent many weeks embroidering a tray cloth for her foster parents. One day, when her foster mother was ill in bed, the child took up her lunch on a tray. She asked for a chocolate from the bedside table and was refused. She then ran from the room and cut up the tray cloth into tiny bits. The worker helped the foster parents to make sense out of what was to them nonsense, explaining that Jennifer's early deprivation, her experience of giving and taking food and being refused this, her great anxiety when her carer was ill had resulted in her expressing infantile, primitive feelings of revenge.

On another occasion, a married woman in her thirties became pregnant with her first child which she wished to place for adoption. She had known the worker for a few weeks and insisted that she would need to see her all the time. The worker set limits on her availability and at this the client became very angry and had a temper tantrum. It transpired that the woman had only recently left home, having been very dependent on her mother. She had transferred this role and her dependency to the social worker, who refused to fulfil the client's phantasy that she could do everything for her (Irvine, 1966). If this had not happened the client would never have been given the confidence to care for the child, to gain a sense of competence and withdraw the adoption plan.

Another great benefit of the psychosocial approach lies in *supervising* other people's work or offering *consultancy*. Often workers need to be given an insight into possible explanations for client behaviour which may have upset or confused them. For instance, it may be a sign of a close relationship that suddenly the client does not want to see you after weeks of working well together. One student felt rejected when a single parent, accused of neglecting her child, failed to open the door when the worker called to see why she had not attended the day nursery. They had developed a trusting relationship at the nursery, where the mother's care of her baby had improved under the guidance of the student. The client needed to reveal her negative views of the worker who could then show a continued interest despite this 'rejection'. A good relationship may not be as beneficial as an honest, objective one.

By using some psychodynamic insights in staff and student supervision, there is scope for distrusting the obvious, for looking beyond everyday understanding of events. It helps too if there is reflection of 'How does this client make me feel?' What is happening in the case situation might then be mirrored in the supervisory relationship. Mattinson (1975) has shown how using this counter-transference can aid sensitive interventions. Recently a student working with a couple who had marital problems yawned throughout super-vision and looked very bored with the case. He then remarked that the couple had seemed bored with their relationship and the 'here we go again' reaction to their troubles.

A framework for understanding the psychosocial approach

Theoretical base is that of Freudian personality theory with its emphasis on the ego's adaptive capacities and problem solving. A systems orientation is implied by the psychosocial person-in-situation whole. Important concepts include de-fence mechanisms, resistance and transference.

Problems are either intrapsychic, interpersonal or environ-mental. They can be conscious or unconscious in origin: the 'cause' of a problem, the 'why?' is seen as important.

Goals are to understand and change the person, the situation or both, that is, direct and indirect intervention. Specific, proximate goals help people with sectors of their lives, such as work. Ultimate goals aim for self-understanding.

The client's role is somewhat passive, a patient role almost.

The worker's role is to study, diagnose and treat. This can be viewed as 'omnipotence' inasmuch as the worker shares or does not share understanding of the client's difficulties with him/her. The worker establishes a relationship based on purposeful expression of feeling; acceptance; a non-judgemental attitude; individualisation; client self-determination where possible; confidentiality and controlled emotional involvement: these are the qualities suggested by Biestek (1965) (which form the mnemonic PANICCC!). The relationship is a 'corrective emotional experience' enabling people to work through their feelings about previous unset-tled conflicts.

Techniques Two main treatment methods, sustaining and modifying, are used, dependent on the study of the 'person-in-situation gestalt'. 'Non-reflective' techniques such as ventilation are helpful in supporting the client and modifying environmental stresses; insight-oriented methods, such as clarification and confrontation, are used when there is agreement to modify the person's feelings, thoughts and behaviour.

Case example

A female probation officer was the third person to be assigned the case of Joan who, despite a recommendation for a conditional discharge for her first offence (stealing a giro cheque), was put on probation for two years. Her former probation officers had assessed her as a 'soft touch' for everyone in her street who used her as an unpaid baby-sitter and general dog's-body.

Joan was nineteen, unemployed and the eldest of a large, working-class family living in poverty. Following her mother's death when she was eleven, her father had remarried and had five more children. Joan and her stepmother were not close; the latter frequently borrowed and did not repay money lent by her stepdaughter. The two of them competed for the father's attention. The client had stolen the cheque on behalf of an older woman friend and had not gained personally from her crime. Joan seemed to have a low opinion of herself, was unkempt and looked about thirteen years old.

Unlike her colleagues, the new worker made no attempt to encourage the girl to leave home. In the initial phase she explored with Joan her preconceptions of what would happen in the relationship, based on her contact with the previous workers. Transference elements in the current of feelings between them revealed that the client had phantasies of control and dependency on the worker. These fears were brought into the open. Negative, ambivalent feelings, which are natural in referred cases, were eased by clarifying the purpose of the meetings and the way the service could help. Motivation was increased by the worker's plan to ask for a discharge of the order three months hence. The goals were for

Joan to achieve greater self-regard, a firmer sense of personal identity and to make more realistic judgements of people.

Joan felt irrationally guilty about asserting herself, even when she was arrested for non-payment of the fine: she had entrusted this money to her stepmother, who had spent it. Nevertheless, by offering an accepting relationship to all the family, the worker respected Joan's need to deny temporarily how painful her past and present experiences were. Later, the client felt accepted enough to reveal her hidden feelings of jealousy and anger towards her family, recognising how she dealt with her aggression by being childlike, compliant and apparently stupid in allowing others to exploit her.

The worker consciously used herself as a role model, being a few years older than her client and having a similar background. Joan began to identify with her helper, talking and dressing like her. She revealed her sadness at losing her mother and, she felt, her father. Sustainment through this ventilation of emotional matters released inner ego strengths: the client began to feel optimistic and plan for herself. She achieved 'separation and individuation' that is a sense of being a separate individual from the worker during this middle phase, offering to help her at a camp with youngsters, hoping eventually to get a job with children.

At this time Joan's father bought her a record-player to replace one that had been stolen; his daughter began to reconsider his position, realistically discussing his 'pig-in-the-middle' dilemma. She tackled her stepmother too, though needing to depend again on the worker for support in working out if she was 'good' or 'bad' for insisting on having a changed identity within the home.

The ending phase, although sad for both client and worker, was seen as a chance for establishing autonomy, especially once the supervision order was discharged. Joan was able to assess herself and rediscover her sense of humour, which, since she lived in an area of rising unemployment and deprivation, she would need.

7

Behavioural Social Work

Why is it that behaviour-modification schemes, which often
aim to change simple behaviours, are couched in difficult
language? The terminology can also be confusing and even
contradictory (See Hudson and Macdonald, 1986). We are
fortunate that educators such as Sheldon and Hudson, whose
work is referred to here, have helped to make the concepts
relevant and accessible for social workers. Learning theory,
on which behavioural approaches are based, is a vast, well-
researched field. Therefore the objectives of this chapter will
be limited to describing some of the different types of
learning; these will be illustrated by outlining a child
management/parent training programme while cognitive
therapy will be examined by means of a case example.
Assertion training is another effective behavioural method,
but will be dealt with in the chapter on working with groups.
To conclude, a theoretical framework will summarise the
main ideas of behavioural approaches to social work.

Before we proceed, though, it is necessary to explore *what
is meant by 'learning'*: it is a process by which behaviour is
modified as the result of experience. It need not be 'correct'
learning – we can learn bad habits as well as good. Equally,
attitudes and emotions can be learned, as well as knowledge
and skills. Technically, learning represents new connections
between stimuli (any sensation) and responses (any element
of behaviour).

Not all behaviour is learned. Certain response tendencies
such as reflexes exist at birth. Even complex behaviour such
as protecting offspring may, as has been shown with some
animals, be innate. Similarly, children develop new skills
such as climbing stairs: this seems to be more a product of

physical maturation than a function of specific learning experiences (Mussen *et al.*, 1969). Nevertheless much of our behaviour is dependent on learning and some of the different procedures are analysed below.

Four different types of learning

There are at least four fundamental classes of learning which are called respondent, operant, observational and cognitive. Hudson and Macdonald (1986) advise us not to worry too much that the first two share many similarities and contradictions; they inter-relate and overlap and are a source of controversy even amongst experts. Though behavioural approaches are in opposition to psychoanalytic methods, discussed in the previous chapter, there are advantages to using them. The worker and the client do not need to guess or infer the meaning of behaviour in order to bring about change. As with task-centred work there is an emphasis on solving current, specific, overt problems; attempts are made to evaluate progress; there is no need to look for a 'cause' and observing why problems arise is less important than what, in the environment, is maintaining 'symptoms' or behaviour.

1. *Respondent conditioning* This form of learning occurs as a response to a stimulus, S $\longrightarrow$ R. It is also known as Pavlovian or classical conditioning (Thomas, 1970). An example is that of anxiety where a previously neutral cue, such as a shop, serves to elicit fear and avoidance, leading to agoraphobia. Interventions usually focus on the respondent behaviour; thus systematic desensitisation procedures encourage responses which are incompatible with anxiety (for example, relaxation and assertion) in the face of an anxiety-provoking stimulus. Just as behaviour can be learned, so it can be unlearned. This process of extinction, of losing a fear by repeated exposure to it, is also known as counter-conditioning or reciprocal inhibition, terms which may be met in further reading. The client is helped to construct an anxiety hierarchy of situations, from those they find easy to those which are very upsetting. While the client relaxes, each situation is progressively imagined up the 'ladder' of feeling,

with the client trying to keep calm (that is, repeatedly pairing a new coping response with a stimulus which previously aroused unpleasant emotions.) However, real-life testing, starting with the most difficult item, has been found to be just as effective (Marks *et al.*, 1971). This used to be known as 'implosive' therapy or 'flooding'. An example of this came from a psychiatric social work friend of mine. He had a client who was 'thrown in the deep end' but who was dramatically helped by what might appear to be a risky method. The worker, relying on a secure and trusting relationship, accompanied the client, who had a fear of dirt, into the local park where they handled dog faeces. Recovery was rapid, thank goodness!

Aversion therapy is an older method of dealing with respondent conditioning, for example in the treatment of sexual deviations (Feldman, 1966). Some methods involve delivering mild electric shocks. This is obviously not a technique likely to be used by social workers, not least because of its ethical implications. More familiar help, especially to those working in Child Guidance, is the use of a bell and pad to treat bedwetting. This involves pairing the two responses of (a) waking and (b) learning to contract the bladder, namely 'holding on' (Lask and Lask, 1981).

2. *Operant conditioning* This occurs when a person's response operates to bring about a reward. This form of learning, according to Sheldon (1984) was demonstrated by Skinner, who showed that a response which produces a reward will become stronger whilst one which does not will become weaker. Often the specific behaviour occurs by chance and is shaped, just as a sculptor manipulates a lump of clay, by continually rewarding those acts which come closer and closer to desired behaviour, that is, 'successive approximations' (Pervin, 1975). A therapist working with autistic children may immediately reward a spontaneous movement which resembles an appropriate social response (providing the child pays attention!) To confuse matters a little, 'shaping' is both respondent and operant conditioning.

Operant behaviour forms the bulk of social work attention and is known as the 'ABC' of behavioural work (Herbert, 1985). This stands for:

Antecedents	Behaviour	Consequences
Child asked to clear away toys	Cooperates	Praised

Positive reinforcement is the most familiar of the procedures which can take the form of social or tangible rewards such as smiles, praise, attention or money. Thomas (1970) likens the term 'reinforcement' to the idea of 'support'. (From a behavioural perspective, Hollis's sustaining techniques, listed in Chapter Six, could be classed as social or tangible rewards.) An important aspect of giving reinforcers is that they should be given immediately and consistently until desired behaviour is occurring and then they should be thinned out gradually (Hudson and Macdonald, 1986).

Chaining and backward chaining are operant procedures used to teach new behaviours and have been successful in work with mentally handicapped people (Tsoi and Yule, 1982). Teaching self-help skills, such as dressing, firstly requires a task analysis of each progressive step to be followed to achieve the required behaviour. For instance, backward chaining was used by foster parents to teach their mentally handicapped foster son how to make his bed. The foster mother handled all but the last link in the chain, then reinforced by rewarding the child for carrying out the last step of tucking in the sheet. Then the last two links of the chain of bedmaking were left for him to master, and so on backwards. He eventually gained the satisfaction of fully completing the tasks himself.

A frequent error made by students is to mix up the term 'negative reinforcement' with 'punishment'. The former is a way of strengthening desired behaviour by removing something undesirable. I usually use the example of putting on sunglasses to avoid the glare! In a juvenile treatment centre the worker, faced with a rowdy group, threatened to detain them beyond four o'clock, unless they quietly sat down. They did so to avoid the unpleasant consequences. This strategy is not as welcome as positively rewarding behaviour, but is preferable to using punishment which is a procedure for decreasing a type of behaviour: it does little to increase new behaviour and punishments, such as shouting, can inadvertently become rewarding (any attention may be deemed better than none). Nevertheless some methods, such as 'fining' adolescents who break family agreements, can be effective, particularly if they are coupled with rewards when the youngster does stick to the rules (see Open University, 1982).

Extinction helps someone to unlearn behaviour by cutting off reinforcers which keep the behaviour going. Whining in a ten-year-old was extinguished by staff in a residential home ignoring this and reinforcing quietness with bubbles and a mirror, which the child loved. 'Time out', (that is, from reinforcement) is an extinction procedure familiar to teachers and parents and is detailed later in this chapter; some parents remove themselves into 'time out', rather than move the child into a corner or another room, and this is just as effective.

It is as well to remember that sometimes it is the setting which could be maintaining problem behaviour. Thus incontinence in elderly person's homes may be partly due to the environment, (high toilets, slippery floors and so on.) Changing the setting sometimes changes the behaviour (See Browne, 1978).

3. *Observational learning* Bandura's Social Learning Theory (1977) emphasised the processes of learning by observation and modelling. The main difference from the previous two types of learning is that reinforcement is not viewed as essential. It is a kind of 'learning at a distance', just as children casually copy adult behaviour. Alternatively, modelling can be more deliberate: social work students may learn by following written or verbal instructions or by imitating the skills of their practice teachers. A common type of observational learning is through the use of role-play in social skills training with psychiatric patients (Trower *et al.*, 1978). As we saw in the last chapter social workers may consciously or otherwise provide a model of coping to their clients; imitative learning is even more likely when there is a positive relationship or when the worker is perceived as competent or of high status (Jehu, 1975).

4. *Cognitive learning* Traditionally, learning theory has concerned itself with outward behaviour, not an 'inner man'. However, people think and solve problems through mental

processes, not only by trial and error. The way we think can influence our feelings and behaviour, as well as the other way around. Cognitive therapy has been used with depressed patients whose moods have been affected by 'learned helplessness' (Seligman, 1975), the belief that they could do nothing to improve their situation. Beck (1976) has had a major influence in this field by altering patients' negative views of themselves, their situations and their prospects. Behaviour change similarly has been achieved by altering 'inner speech', the way we talk to ourselves (Meichenbaum, 1978). Cognitive behaviour change is analysed in the case example; the other types of learning below.

A child management/parent training programme

For many years child management techniques have been taught to parents whose children have been 'driving them up the wall!' These methods highlight the theories of respondent, operant and imitative learning in action. Parents have been taught to change children's behaviour by altering the way they handle them. The experiences reported by Scott (1983) are summarised to show how down-to-earth and relevant behavioural approaches can be.

Scott worked with individuals and groups, the latter encouraging anxious parents to relax through the exchange of humorous anecdotes. The parent groups were popular and successful and were conducted on the following lines. After completing a child behaviour inventory, each parent was able to assess the rate and frequency of up to thirty-six problem categories. The most common difficulties were non-compliance – the child simply ignoring parental commands. Parents were taught consistency. Often a child gets a treat just because mum or dad is in a good mood; in this way behaviour becomes divorced from its consequences. The groups were taught to spell out exactly what behaviour they wanted and what the reward would be, by the use of the 'when . . . then' technique. Thus, 'When you have cleared away your toys, then you can watch TV.' Children may not be used to this and could become abusive, therefore parents were taught 'planned ignoring'. Rather than be drawn into a (reinforcing) row, parents rehearse walking at least three feet away from the child; showing no expression; avoiding discussion except to restate if need be, 'When you have calmed down, then we will talk about it'. Members reinforced each other's attempts to persevere.

The next technique demonstrated (and role played) was how to use praise. Rather than nagging, parents were asked to spot when the child was being good, indeed doing anything other than the problem behaviour. Then praise was to be given, looking at the child; moving to within three feet and smiling; putting an arm around the child and voicing approval within five seconds of seeing the good behaviour. Behaviour, not the child was praised, for example, 'That's very good of you, playing quietly while mummy reads.' Teaching new skills, like catching a ball or threading a needle, came next: the parents were shown how to give specific instructions, how to assist the child or show her/him exactly what to do. Praise was to be given for any small improvement and this strengthened their relationship, so that the use of 'time out', taught next, was more likely to work.

Undesired behaviours were to be treated by 'time out', (that is, from reinforcement) within seconds of their occurring. Parents were told to give the child warning and reasons for doing this. Taking the child to a 'time out' area, such as the corner of a room with no distractions, was to last for not more than three to five minutes; other procedures involved moving at least three feet away and avoiding replying to the 'It's not fair' type of arguments. How to use 'fines and penalties', particularly with older children who broke agreements and thereby forfeited privileges, was the final topic taught to parents. Some parents, afraid of abusing their children, have been taught extra techniques of 'anger control': this is a combination of using distractions, WASP (Wait, Absorb, Slowly Proceed) and other 'self-talk' devices. These have also helped husbands who batter to regain self-control (Saunders, 1984).

Hudson and Macdonald warn that research into all these behavioural techniques is not yet wholly convincing, yet they can at least offer us a broader way of thinking about problems

(Hudson and Macdonald, 1986). The same is true of cognitive therapy which was used in the following referral.

Case example

Mr Lin was a fifty-year-old, happily married man with grown up children. He was twice made redundant and as he was about to return to employment he became depressed. He was referred to a psychiatric day hospital where he was seen by a student social worker who had studied cognitive therapy. It emerged that the client had been experiencing an array of problems – behavioural, cognitive, affective and physical. His symptoms included depression, feelings of unreality, fears of dying and loss of confidence (Hudson, 1982).

The student explained about anxiety management techniques (Meichenbaum, 1978) and cognitive therapy (Beck, 1976). They agreed to meet weekly and follow these programmes, with Mr Lin completing the homework tasks in between, that is, practising and recording his thoughts and successes, and learning to relax with an audiotape. Many of the sessions involved role-playing behavioural tasks, such as waiting for and getting on a bus. The student frequently introduced stressful material while teaching the client how to breathe properly and relax: leaflets and hand-outs on coping with anxiety and negative thoughts were read out aloud in the session and given to Mr Lin to keep, so as to prompt and reinforce self-management efforts.

Anxiety management techniques included reminding the client that his feelings of faintness and palpitations did not mean he was about to have a heart attack: they are the body's normal reactions to stress and tension and are not dangerous in themselves. He laughingly admitted that he had never fainted and, when encouraged to visualise a feared event and become tense, he recognised how his body reacted. He was taught to wait for the fear to pass, not to fight or give way to it, to 'just accept it'. Mr Lin realised that his fear faded if he stopped adding to it with the fear of fear itself. Regular practice at home confirmed this and he looked more hopeful with each week that passed, although the worker gave him a message to 'go slow' and to expect setbacks, saying 'Welcome these as an extra chance to practise.' The word 'practise' was underlined and distinguished from the word 'test'. The latter is daunting and can result in clients brooding on 'failure' rather than accepting that there will be good and bad days.

The relaxation exercise used in the sessions involved the client and worker lying on the floor and saying out loud several times statements such as, 'My hands are heavy and warm', 'My feet and legs are heavy and warm', 'My heartbeat is calm and regular' (ten times) and so on. These simple ideas helped the client (and worker) to feel refreshed.

When using cognitive therapy the worker explained to Mr Lin that people are upset, not so much by events, but the view that they take of them. This is essentially an educative approach which prompts people to write down rational responses to negative, automatic thoughts (those that simply 'pop up'). To generate hope a leaflet giving case histories of successfully treated patients was read, plus a card to carry around, listing the most common negative assumptions. These are *all or nothing* thinking: seeing everything in black and white; *overgeneralisation*: expecting constant bad luck: *mental filter*: dwelling on the bad and filtering out the positive; *automatic discounting*: brushing aside compliments; *jumping to conclusions*: reading minds, 'He looks down on me' and fortune-telling, 'The future will be a disaster'; *magnification and minimisation*: the binocular trick of magnifying your imperfections and shrinking your strengths; *emotional reasoning*: 'I feel bad. I am bad'; feelings are not facts; *should statements*: 'I should do this' makes you feel guilty instead of getting you to do something; *labelling and mislabelling*: you are not a 'failure', you made a 'mistake'; *personalisation*: makes us blame ourselves for whatever happens or whatever others do.

Mr Lin could identify with the idea that he had been picking on himself instead of being gentle on his imperfections; he had done some carpentry which was unsatisfactory, but not a disaster. He learned to 'catch' the negative thoughts which made him feel depressed. He learned to question the validity and consistency of these, to test out hypotheses that he could not enjoy anything, by setting up 'experiments' of events he used to find enjoyable, and to congratulate himself for making an effort. Mr Lin's diary, which he had been asked to keep, showed a lifting of mood and an increasing number of activities found pleasurable.

Scott and Ross (1986) have positively evaluated these therapies. The ultimate test, of course, is whether behaviour actually changes (Sheldon, 1984). This was certainly true for Mr Lin, despite the 'placebo' effect of the worker's optimism and empathic relationship, which doubtless played a part. To conclude the chapter and summarise the fundamentals of behavioural social work, a framework for understanding theory and practice is offered.

A framework for understanding behavioural approaches

Theoretical base is Learning Theory, including Respondent, Operant, Observational and Cognitive Theories.

Problems such as habits, anxiety, depression, obsessions (or behavioural deficiencies such as lacking social skills) are measured in terms of frequency, intensity, duration and context.

Goals must be specific, observable (or self-reported, for example, sexual problems), concrete and stated in behavioural terms.

The client's role. The person must be helped to be motivated or the agent, a parent for instance, must want change to occur. Diaries and records are usually kept to aid a behavioural assessment of the ABC of behaviours or baseline measures from which 'before and after' measures can be taken (see Sheldon, 1983). The client's view of what is a reward is vital.

The worker's role is to listen and observe carefully, to assess assets, resources and the environment. A list of problems and goals and the selection of an initial focus is agreed upon. The ABC of behaviours is measured, a strategy decided and evaluated on completion. The worker offers hope and a genuine, concerned relationship.

Techniques involve systematic desensitisation procedures, extinction, shaping, positive reinforcement, chaining, negative reinforcement, punishment, modelling, role rehearsal, self-regulation and the education of other agents, such as teachers, parents and colleagues.

8

Family Work

Working with families and children is a high priority for social services departments (Parsloe and Stevenson, 1978). Many of the referrals continue to be connected with the plague of poverty and the rationing of resources (Jordan, 1974). Other reasons for referral, sometimes by families themselves but more usually from other sources, are concerned with problems rooted within family relationships. This aspect will be the focus of this chapter.

For some years social work with families was known as 'family casework' but if ever the whole family was seen, this was intended to better the welfare of one of its members. In the past twenty years, 'family therapy' has become a popular approach, but this is more than doing 'casework with more people in the room'; it is used when the whole family is the target. Problem behaviour in one or more members is thought to be both a cause and a consequence of family interaction. How people get along with one another and, more fundamentally, how the family solves its problems, is seen as important in preventing dysfunction.

Although this chapter will concentrate on family therapy, I have deliberately chosen not to give it that title: the clinical term 'therapy' may be off-putting; those who have not studied the techniques feel like outsiders and there is a misconception that family therapy can only be undertaken with specific problems and technological apparatus. The relevance of this method in social services departments has been discussed elsewhere (Coulshed and Abdullah-Zadeh, 1983). Suffice it here to say that, despite those who would make 'precious' the knowledge and skills, there is scope for practical intervention in many settings (Treacher and Carpenter, 1984). The use of

87

this approach can help families to draw on their own problem-solving strengths; with humanity and humility in the family therapy movement (Walrond-Skinner, 1979) the development of theory and practice will bequeath to the future yet more creative insights and effective strategies for change. A few of them are dealt with here, but the field is so 'advanced' that continuous study is required. The chapter will conclude by looking at work with one family, plus a theoretical framework which will summarise the main ideas.

Understanding family dynamics

The diversity of family life from a race, structure and class perspective is well documented (see Rapoport *et al.*, 1982). It is impossible to talk about a 'conventional' family: each is unique in its patterns of behaviour, communication and values. Therefore the task for the social worker is to understand: 'How does *this* family work?'

One common mistake is to assume that clients' kin are like one's own. Many people grow up in a family setting and unless we look at the influence this has had on the way we love and work – the two main tasks of life (Scherz, 1970) there is a danger of unknowingly trying to replicate our own experiences with client families. A skilled colleague of mine, one of three brothers, was working with a family of the same composition; unwittingly he behaved as if he were one of the brothers. Whenever I am working with a group where the father stays in a peripheral role, I watch that I do not recreate a mirror image of my own family's functioning. Before working intensively with families, then, it is necessary to work out your own attitudes and beliefs about family life (Bowen, 1978).

Trying to understand a family is like jumping onto a moving bus. You have the disadvantage of being a temporary passenger on their journey through life, with people leaving and joining along the way. It is a complex business, seeing how a family (like the individual coping with developmental crises, which we reviewed in Chapter Four) has to go through a number of transitions. Each of these requires the group to restructure its operations while at the same time providing continuity to its members. Gorell Barnes (1984) deals with this *family life cycle*, giving a clear account of how we may leave home, achieve independence, become half of a couple, form a family with children, launch these to leave an 'empty nest' and then, possibly, move back into a dependent stage in later life. The changes which are required in the family as a whole are very demanding. These are made even more so as every member is probably struggling with different stages all at the same time. Thus, whilst the family has to let go of its youngsters, it has to accept newcomers; it has to make space for different needs, renegotiating all the time the numerous patterns of relationship between people.

Every family can be placed at one of three possible points on a spectrum from flexibility through rigidity to chaos (Gorrell Barnes, 1984). If a family can 'bend' with its changing shape and processes, then it avoids the problems of engaging in perpetual uncertainty and disagreement or failing to adapt to new needs. In social services, we see families who are having trouble redefining rules for children who are moving into adolescence; or disorganised families who fail to see that each generation has its own boundaries. In a day nursery recently, I saw a parent competing for the baby's toys.

To recapitulate: as well as understanding where the family is in its life cycle evolution, it helps to observe if *family hierarchy* is being maintained or if generational *boundaries* are crossed, as above. Difficulties can also arise if relationships are too close or too distant – what Minuchin (1974) calls 'enmeshment' or 'disengagement'. When I dealt with a fourteen-year-old boy, referred for delinquent activities, I noticed that he and his single parent mother were very close; he helped to care for a younger brother and sister and had adult responsibilities. He objected to coming home at a reasonable time in the evening and seemed confused as to which generation and hierarchy he belonged to. I had avoided going blindly into the interview by speculating that, as this was the parent's first attempt at rearing a teenager, perhaps she was unsure how to treat him, as adult or child; perhaps, too, family rules needed renegotiating to provide the boy with more space and privacy.

Another tool which can be useful for planning ahead, for

use with a family or to aid a case presentation is the *family tree* or genogram. The symbols can be easily mastered so that a 'road map' of relationship can be clearly seen. See Figure 8.1.

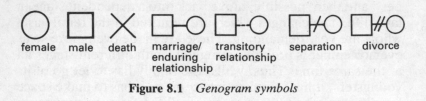

Figure 8.1   *Genogram symbols*

The family just described is represented in Figure 8.2.

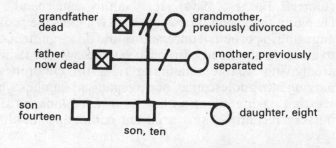

Figure 8.2   *Illustrative genogram*

Burnham (1986) gives further examples of less straightforward family trees, (for example, showing what is known as 'blended' step families). In understanding family dynamics, perhaps the most important concept to grasp is the ability to think of the family as a system. Because I believe that this involves a difficult mental leap, it is explored in some detail below.

The family as an open system in transformation

We saw, in Chapter Six, that the uniqueness of each individual's personality derives from inner and outer experiences. Sometimes, when we work with individuals, we find that forces in their environment prevent change taking place or that these forces undo our efforts once the person returns to the context in which difficulties arose. I inspected a large file in an agency which had dealt with a 'multi-problem family' for twenty years. Despite enormous programmes of individual change, none of the children had literally, or psychologically managed to leave home: their problem behaviour simply returned once they were back in the family fold.

To understand this we have to see the family as a small organisation with its own hierarchical patterns, rules, decision-making procedures, lines of communication, controls and so on. (The main differences from an actual organisation are that families have biological links, cannot choose membership and usually have a shared history and future.) It is only by 'joining' an organisation that we learn about its invisible rules. These govern who talks to whom about what; how arguments are resolved; which topics are taboo (the elephant in the corner which no one mentions), who belongs to which subgroups and how life outside with other social networks is managed. We will look at techniques for 'joining' families later, for without this engagement no change will take place.

If we view the family as a system we see that members affect and are affected by one another: they interact, are interdependent and maintain balance (homeostasis) by regulating the limits of change. Walrond-Skinner (1976) uses the game of chess as an analogy: each chess piece has certain properties but these can change, depending on the particular situation on the board at any point in time. So sometimes the queen is all-powerful and the pawns in a weaker position, but this situation can change if there is a different configuration amongst the other pieces. It becomes difficult, therefore, to talk about 'strict' mothers or 'passive' fathers as if these were fixed attributes rather than the actions and reactions of people in relation to their specific circumstances.

Families maintain and protect themselves by developing, possibly over generations, particular rules about the pattern of interactions, which require transformation during the life cycle. These patterns become autonomous and repetitive, despite individual differences. They are so integrated that no one is aware of them (yet they have to be spotted so that they might be rearranged). A married couple repeatedly rowed, triggered by predictable words and actions. They temporarily 'forgot their lines' in front of a counsellor. Their customary interchanges and rhythm were soon back on course when the husband remarked, 'You are supposed to say . . .'!

Hence people get stuck with their difficulties which are often the result of normal, foreseeable crises. But sometimes service may only be given if a label, such as 'violent family' is attached; there is a danger thereby that agencies over-react and themselves become part of the problem. Equally, families themselves perpetuate difficulties by trying solutions which then become part of a problem spiral. We have to learn to see the family 'dance' (Minuchin and Fishman, 1981) and steer them out of never-ending habits by trying out new solutions or experiences, perhaps in our actual sessions with them. A systems view of family dynamics requires that we see the sequences of interaction not in a linear but in a circular fashion. Rather than accept as 'reality' that:

> wife is angry → therefore husband goes to the pub

or:

> husband goes to the pub → therefore wife gets angry

we need to 'bend' the arrows and see that:

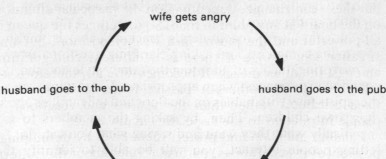

A social worker who practises seeing events in this 'whole' or systems way will hesitate to blame, take sides or give easy explanations for the 'cause' of such difficulties – none of which would lead anywhere, in any case. Rather, each person is viewed as part of a circular system of action and reaction which can begin and end at any point ('punctuation' is the technical word for this). No one 'gains' or is a 'victim'. There is thus little point in asking, 'Who started it?' However one problem with this circular view of causality is that it ignores the current unresolved power issues between men and women in our society, which are reflected in family relationships. A gender-sensitive worker could, nevertheless, help a couple where there is a power imbalance by showing how both are caught by society's expectations, but that, if they wish, they have the power and the potential to choose to change (see Pilalis and Anderton, 1986).

Beginning family work

Gorell Barnes (1984) and Burnham (1986) give useful examples of 'selling lines' and letters to attract families and convince them of the need for a family approach. Then it is vital to begin properly, engaging everyone in the group, confirming their importance in helping you to help them. Taking care over this 'social stage' (Haley, 1976), being courteous and getting to know everyone, is time well spent. Joining operations do not include confronting them with your 'truth' about their difficulties: the worker deliberately blends with the family to see how it works (but as a coach, not as a member of the team).

Minuchin (1974) recommends 'tracking', that is, making approving comments and asking clarifying questions as well as 'mirroring' tactics of adopting the family style and sharing common experiences, when appropriate. For instance, some therapists play with babies on the floor and tell families about their own children. Then, by asking the members to say specifically what they want and saying what you can do, by letting people interact, you will be able to identify the problem: not working too hard and relaxing helps you to watch the process of the interview, alongside listening to the content. Moving too quickly, aiming too high and feeling responsible for the family's difficulties are erroneous features of beginners' work. It helps to stick to mundane themes which will emerge, no matter how 'bizarre' the presenting problem.

In a family where the son had attacked his stepfather with a knife, within minutes the issue centred on who could switch TV channels without consulting anyone else. Rather than dwell on the violent event the worker focused on these key themes of control and concern for others, which lay at the heart of all the problems. Signs that the family do not want the problem solved, 'We want to change but we want to stay the same', may become apparent. Then ask yourself, or the family, 'What effect does this problem have on each individual?' or 'What would happen if the problem was solved?' Sometimes the problem is functional, as opposed to dysfunctional, in that it keeps the family 'in balance' – a case of 'Better the Devil you know. . . .?'

Categories of intervention for family change are numerous and thus are best illustrated through the case example and a summary of the four methods and models, with the expectation that further study will aid familiarity with some of family therapy's more esoteric ideas.

Four methods of family work

Methods span psychoanalytic family approaches (see Box *et al.*, 1981); structural work (Minuchin, 1974); behavioural (see Crowe, 1982) and strategic/systemic therapies (Haley, 1976; Palazzoli *et al.*, 1980).
1. *Psychoanalytic* models incorporate family myths, influences over generations and interlocking pathology – how children, for example, might be drawn into marital projections (Mainprice, 1974). The use of the family tree; family sculpting (using a *tableau vivant* to express emotional ties; Walrond-Skinner, 1976); seeing problems as a reflection of deeper conflicts and interpreting these, are appropriate methods of helping.
2. *Structural* work is based on present transactions, often

challenging and checking what occurs in the session or asking families to enact their difficulties. Positive labelling (the 'O.K.' principle) is a first step to change: thus an 'overprotective' parent is seen as 'concerned'. This method concentrates on what people do rather than how they feel, since the first step is to change how they treat one another.

3. *Behavioural* family therapists focus on current 'symptoms': in couples work communications skills (see Gott man *et al.*, 1977) empathy development and reciprocity negotiation ('tit for tat') are some of the behaviours taught.

4. *Strategic* work emphasises 'reframing' in order to shift a family's view of its problems. A family were bitterly disappointed because they had failed to reach a foster child whom they asked to be removed. It was necessary for me to point out that often it is the case that foster children do not get attached in case they break up the family strength and closeness. The *Strategic/Systemic* approach introduces further ideas about team helping, hypothesising on how the family interlink as a system and the necessity for workers to remain objective (Palazzoli *et al.*, 1980). The following intervention drew on some of these methods.

Case example

Sue, thirteen, had not been to school for a year. The school social worker had never seen her as Sue refused to come downstairs during home visits. A psychiatric assessment was planned, but the family, which included three older sisters who had all left home, agreed instead to work as a group. A male colleague and myself saw them at home on four occasions. Prior to contact, we hypothesised from the family tree and life cycle stage that Sue was coping with adolescent challenges whilst her parents faced re-forming as a couple and prepared for the prospect of an 'empty nest'. As the father was a long-distance lorry driver, mother and daughter were probably close and maybe Sue's symptom was linked to the system's crossed hierarchical and generational boundaries.

Although under subtle pressure to begin work without father, we never did so: we took off our coats, drank tea and waited to begin the formal business once he arrived. We showed we were 'with' them and would be neutral. Sometimes merely bringing a whole family together is powerful enough to unblock communications or prevent their being diverted, for example, through a child. Sue never spoke. She looked boyish and kept her head bowed, but her mother revealed that once this youngest daughter was grown up she planned to leave her husband. We confronted these themes of growing up and leaving home suggesting, 'Perhaps Sue is sacrificing her growing up to save the family from splitting up?'

We used 'circular questioning' (Penn, 1982) to highlight different viewpoints and introduce new information about how each third party viewed relations between two others. We asked, 'When your mother rows with your father, what does Sue do?' and 'Who will be most, (and least) upset when your mother leaves home?'

A clear boundary around the daughters' subsystem was drawn by asking their parents' permission to see the sisters privately to set 'homework'. We asked the older sisters to confide in Sue what it was like growing up: their parents agreed not to ask about the 'secret' task. Between visits Sue enjoyed these sisterly get-togethers and, after six weeks, she returned to school, where she did well. Her parents remained married. (Currently, there is criticism that workers are perpetuating the role of women in families (Pilalis and Anderton, 1986). This is an important argument for you to pursue and to be aware of in your practice.)

A framework for understanding family work

Theoretical base is systems theory. Important concepts include structure, hierarchy, boundaries, homeostasis and interactional sequences within the family.

Problems are rooted within the family relationships which may be presented as one member's problems. Communication may be blocked, distorted or displaced through the 'sympton bearer'. Family myths and secrets may carry over from generation to generation. Life cycle crises force a transformation of the family's implicit rules for interaction within and outside the family group – problems arise around the need to readjust and adapt.

Goals are to 'join' the family in order to restructure interactional patterns; to free the 'identified patient' and help the family to use its strengths to solve the problem by reorganising boundaries, altering inflexible roles and so on.

The client's role. The family is the client, the target for change and the system which acts to change its own dynamics and ways of doing things, aided by the worker who helps them to stick to particular themes which give a 'slice of family life'. Where possible, the whole family and anyone significant for problem solving, attend sessions, which are usually time-limited.

The worker's role. There may be two workers as co-therapists or a therapeutic team who hypothesise as to how the family system is affecting or being affected by the presenting problem. The workers do not take sides, blame or challenge the family's view of the problem, but sustain the group as it attempts to change its patterns of interaction, its 'dance'.

Techniques are numerous, including joining and restructuring moves such as 'tracking'; mirroring; increasing intensity; working with detail; observing the process in the room; confirming family competence; enacting the sequence of actions around the problem area; creating space and changing boundaries; setting tasks, and taking 'time out' with colleagues to plan strategic questions and manoeuvres so that the family experience their relationships and their difficulties from a different perspective. From the beginner's point of view, the microskills related to each stage of the interview might include the following:

1. *Social Stage*   Ask the family to sit where they wish if it is an office interview; introduce yourself; speak to each person and get to know their name; check if anyone who should be present is missing; prevent discussion of the

problem until everyone has been introduced; note the seating, mood, the way they deal with you and each other; clarify what you know of their situation and why you have asked them all to come.

2. *Problem Stage*   Ask what is the problem or how you can help or what changes they want. Listen to everyone's views without making interpretations or offering advice or trying to get them to see the problem your way. Make sure everyone gets a turn, respect their view of the situation; be in charge but do not take over the problem solving, watch the reaction of listeners. Obtain specific information on 'Who does what when?' in relation to the actual problem. Use circular questioning to look at alliances and differences amongst members' view of the difficulties.

3. *Interaction Stage*   If family members begin to talk to one another about the problem do not stop this; watch as they show you their way of solving problems. Otherwise direct people to talk to one another, bringing in other people to comment on what is happening or to help sort out conflicts. Keep the focus on the problem and their ideas for solution.

4. *Ending Stage*   Set homework tasks after agreeing the nature of the problem and goals. Decide time-limits. Say goodbye to everyone.

9

Working with Groups

Thus far, except for family therapy, the methods outlined in
previous chapters have been used to help clients mainly on a
one-to-one basis. Some writers view family therapy as
groupwork (Zastrow, 1985) but, to me, there are sufficient
differences, in methods if not concepts, to treat the
approaches separately. This chapter will introduce and clarify
some of the principles and practice of groupwork. My
experience is in helping groups of elderly people but, more
recently, I have engaged in 'indirect' work, acting as a
facilitator in groups with nurses and residential social workers. Also, in teaching groupwork to students, I have used the
class experientially as 'the group' (Coulshed, 1987); examples
from these, together with observations from running assertion training groups, will illustrate group programme and
process. Whether you are working directly with clients in
groups or with staff and others on their behalf (for example,
as a team leader/manager) you will find that small groups are
similar in development and behaviour. These processes,
together with the leader's tasks at each stage, will be
described.

None of us is new to groups. Nevertheless, even though we
might belong to work, leisure, religious and neighbourhood
groups, some people seem to doubt their ability actually to do
groupwork. One phantasy is that members will refuse to
cooperate, challenge our authority or dissolve into chaos. It is
suggested that if we enjoy group membership we are more
likely to use this approach (A. Brown, 1986). Whilst there are
no guarantees for running successful groups, there are ways
of increasing the likelihood that you and the members enjoy
and gain from the experience: some of these ingredients for
effective groupwork will be considered.

99

Why use groupwork?

Social workers often say that they 'should' be doing group-work (Whitaker, 1975). The only justifiable reason for doing so is that it is the best method for helping the people concerned. Groups do have their disadvantages, not least that some individuals are frightened of them. Having experienced tyranny in one group to which I belonged, I would hesitate to include anyone whose self-esteem was at a low ebb. Great care has to be taken in selecting members and, indeed, a sensitive and skilful leader. Other points to bear in mind are that groups are extremely time-consuming: clients, colleagues and the agency might present obstacles either before or after you start; then there is the added worry of putting your competence and the outcome at stake. Additionally, you have to be very organised (and healthy) since it is not easy to postpone a session. (Twice I have had to conduct groups following funerals.)

In spite of drawbacks, groups offer many 'curative factors' not available through individual helping methods. They can be a source of power for clients pressing for social change; mutual information, support and hope are also available. Groups give an opportunity for learning and testing interpersonal and social skills, a sense of belonging and 'being in the same boat' which is reassuring; there is a chance to use the leader or other members as role models; the chance to get feedback about coping attempts is possible in groups and, perhaps most importantly, there is scope to help as well as to be helped (Yalom, 1970).

Models of groupwork

It is possible to categorise models and methods of groupwork in various ways and, because they tend to overlap, the classifications could be confusing. A well known way of classifying in terms of the aims of groupwork is that employed by Papell and Rothman (1966). They distinguish three models – remedial, reciprocal amd social goals: these aim respectively for individual assessment, support or change; group support, change or education and, finally, environmental change. Besides categorising by aims, models may emphasise different theoretical orientations (for instance, behavioural); problem types (for instance, drug abuse); clientele (for instance women only) or time (for instance, short- or long-term groups).

A tidy list of six models for groupwork practice has been drawn up by A. Brown (1986). He suggests:

1. *Peer confrontation groups* which operate by peer pressure, openness and support. The Minnesota Method of treating drug users is one example, which operates similarly to Glasser's Reality Therapy (1965). I joined a highly confronting 'Seven Steps to Freedom' group in a Canadian prison: as part of pre-release work, non-offenders kept prisoners in the 'hot seat', forcing them to take responsibility for their behaviour and contesting all excuses.

2. *Problem-solving, task-centred groups*. In the United Kingdom Priestley *et al.* (1978) help groups to follow a structured procedure for problem solving, operating on similar lines to the task-centred approach, that is, they are dependent on the goals which clients choose.

3. *Psychotherapeutic groups* of which there are many models whose emphases range from pathology to growth. Some, like group dynamic therapy, draw on psychoanalytic theory and focus on intrapersonal and interpersonal feelings and relationships. Specific approaches such as T.A. (transactional analysis), gestalt and psychodrama groups consider human potential but highlight self-discovery rather than group process. Clear overviews of all of these are given by Shaffer and Galinsky (1974) and Garvin (1981).

4. *Self-help groups* emphasise mutual aid and do not necessarily need social work leadership. Examples are Alcoholics Anonymous and community carers support groups, such as those run by the parents of mentally handicapped people or the relatives of psychogeriatric patients (see Masters, 1982).

5. *Human relations training groups* are experiential sensitivity groups which are sometimes available to social work students on training courses. They are also known as 'Training' or 'T' groups (see Cooper, 1981).

6. *Social goals models*, such as youth and community work groups, aim either for practical gains and neighbourhood

resources or to raise the consciousness and skills of participants (see Alinsky, 1972).

To summarise, models and methods of groupwork change
in emphasis as regards:

- the leader or the group as the change agent
- the individual or the group as the target for change
- using individual or group processes to achieve this
- focus on health or 'pathology' of the members
- focus on unconscious or conscious mechanisms
- task achievement or relationship behaviours.

Nevertheless the same group may itself shift emphasis during
its lifetime (McCaughan, 1977).

Sometimes groups never get going and it is difficult to
understand why not. Whitaker (1975) suggests that effectiveness is related to the backing obtained from your organisation, paying attention to structural factors such as group size,
composition and staffing and ensuring consensus about aims
and procedures. The most significant finding in a survey of
sixty-one groups was the divergence of purpose between
workers and members – the latter wanting environmental
changes, the former aiming to change individual behaviour
(Levinson, 1973). Currently one social services department I
know of is planning a group for single parents, ostensibly to
combat isolation; the 'hidden agenda' is to improve parent-
hood skills and so the project's contradictory aims may doom
it to failure from the start.

Success is related to the attention paid to group process,
stage of group development and the leader's interventions
(Carlock and Byrum-Gaw, 1982; Burton, 1983). Following
the energy of the group and moving it towards greater trust,
openness, role-free behaviour and interdependence are
therefore analysed in some detail below.

The stages of group development and the worker's tasks

Most groups evolve through stages of pre-affiliation, power
and control, intimacy, differentiation and separation; a more
popular way of remembering developmental phases is to

name them 'forming: storming, norming, performing and adjourning' (Tuckman and Jensen, 1977).

In the *forming* stage a private idea to start a group becomes public when you see a potential pool of clients whose needs could best be met by working in a group. Decisions have to be made about group purpose, goals, place and duration. The time investment in this planning and intake phase, from presenting a proposal to team colleagues to reaching out and determining membership is immense. You have to make sure that other professionals understand your ideas so that 'unsuitable' people are not referred. Other tasks include decisions about the number of sessions, frequency and length (for example, twelve weekly meetings of one-and-a-half hours); how you will evaluate the input and whether or not to work alone: Pfeiffer and Jones (1975) and Preston-Shoot (1986) posit the pros and cons of co-leadership. Then you have to decide if you need an outside consultant for support (A. Brown, 1984). Group membership can be open or closed (the former can prevent staleness but can also be unstable). Checking if food, transport and equipment will be needed are practical but important jobs also to be undertaken at this stage.

You can then consider group composition; 'homogeneous enough to ensure stability and heterogeneous enough to ensure vitality' is a well established law (Redl, 1951). Size depends on the goals but usually groups in social work need to be more than three and less than fourteen; 'large enough for stimulation, small enough for participation and recognition' (A. Brown, 1986).

Preparatory interviews with each member allow client and worker to screen one another while also ensuring that the nature of the group is consistent with the individual's needs. Some practitioners even give a hand-out incorporating guidelines on how to get the best out of the experience (Corey *et al.*, 1982).

Individual and group aims, the need for attendance and confidentiality are areas for discussion early on. The process of clarifying and negotiating the contract starts in the first session but, since implicit assumptions often emerge later, this may need renegotiating. I once spent most of the early sessions with students on a groupwork course re-examining the aims of our contract. These had been agreed as (a) reading and presenting groupwork theory, (b) role-playing client groups and (c) analysing the dynamics of the student group itself, that is, watching ourselves be a group. Fear among some members led to an adversarial position being adopted: some were eager to try out the methods with clients and then explore their own interpersonal relations and group processes; others preferred to emphasise the theoretical material. Consensus about primary and secondary goals was eventually achieved, due to a willingness to face the conflicts and underlying fears of group disintegration.

Among the skills and tasks of the leader in this forming stage are: acknowledging initial uncertainties; being courteous; learning names (perhaps through a game); giving information (not too much); connecting one person to another – 'Does anybody else feel the same?'; playing the 'absent member' role, (for example, putting into words what members may be wanting to say, but do not want to risk); balancing answering questions with asking members for their views and showing concern for each individual (Northen, 1969).

Exploring and testing are the themes in the *storming* stage when 'Do I belong?' concerns are replaced by 'Do I have any influence?' The group is quite fragile and may not continue if the leadership does not provide enough security while individuals query if they are going to get what they came for. This stage can be draining. There is a need to keep calm in the face of conflicts, openly recognising differences. There may be challenges to your authority ('Do I want to be here? I will not be told what to do') which may or may not stem from ambivalence or transference. At all times the worker must model acceptance, especially towards those who are isolated or other 'deviant' members. A good sense of pacing and timing indicates to the worker when to be structured and orderly and when to be non-directive towards the group so that responsibilities can be released to the membership.

Once some of the issues of power and control have been sorted out, 'Do people like me?' can become a feature of the *norming* stage. Trust, intimacy and cohesion become possible. A 'we' feeling, a growing *ésprit de corps* is signified by high attendance, rituals, such as ownership of seats, putting the group before oneself and exclusivity (which can prevent newcomers joining). People begin to help each other, so that the leader may be less active. Universality of problems and interests can bc drawn out, perhaps through the selection of a high status member to risk exposing feelings (Hartford, 1971). When people perceive that this is a safe thing to do, then others start to talk more openly about themselves. This leads to a sense that 'This is our group': it no longer belongs to the leader.

The evolution of a group culture is possible when *performing* occurs. There is an acting together to solve problems and effect change in the group or some system outside it. One member may be ready to show 'the way things are done here' by modelling behaviour and values for the rest to emulate. This happened in one of my student-training groups where one charismatic member, stereotyped as 'wise, confident and responsible' declared that he was 'fed up' with this role. He confessed that he was often anxious and would like to receive as well as give help to others. His challenge increased everyone's openness and extended role possibilities for all.

The planned termination phase or *adjourning* prevents stagnation and dwindling productivity, which can happen if members or the worker hang on to the group through guilt or uncertainty (Whitaker, 1975). Setting goals for the time left; reviewing experiences; emphasising gains; reinforcing interests outside the groups and recognising feelings of loss are some of the tasks which help. At this point social workers evaluate the sessions and ask for feedback. For instance, I asked one group for one specific thing they had learned about (a) groupwork theory, (b) their own skills and (c) one group event which stood out as significant. In relation to the latter, most remembered the early period of conflict – the 'make or break' turning-point when people began to be truly themselves and they feared the group would end.

To sum up, groups move through individuality to mutuality, then to interdependence and, finally, to independence. The leader's role, accordingly, is, in turn, active, pivotal, peripheral and directive. The worker must let the group energy flow, facilitating, guiding, steering, holding the group to the task, encouraging expressions of difference and sustaining by simply being there (Henry, 1981).

Handling difficulties in groups

Careful selection, preparation and group maintenance may not prevent some members becoming loners, scapegoats, monopolisers, silent or casualties of the group experience. Often such behaviour is functional for the group. Therefore, while individual counselling might help, many of the techniques for handling such difficulties can be put back to the group for their resolution.

In addressing the scapegoat phenomenon, for instance, Shulman (1979) suggests that the worker first observes the pattern, tunes in to her/his own feelings about this, avoids siding with or against the scapegoat and asks the group what is happening. Then the pattern may be pointed out. A non-critical challenge could be put to the group for them to find a way of coping with this process. This lets them think about the need for a scapegoat and also gives the scapegoat time to consider reasons for volunteering for the role.

If the leader does not handle the monopoliser in the group, Yalom (1970) warns that the members will start to absent themselves or explode! The worker could ask the group why it permits such behaviour; ask the monopoliser to persist and then explore the response; ask the group to monitor and give feedback; value what is said but ask others to become 'active' as well; use videotape feedback, or, in a caring, humorous way, use a stop-watch or an egg-timer!

The group is more likely openly to resent a silent member, who they feel could be judging them or not sharing as much. The leader needs to model respect and at the same time convey interest in hearing from silent people. I asked one student who never spoke if she was always a listener in groups. She said, 'I find it hard talking in groups' and agreed that she would like to be different; therefore the group encouraged her to become more confident in expressing her views.

If bizarre behaviour breaks out in the group, members often display remarkable perception and sensitivity; they also want to protect the group from threatened chaos, if psychotic behaviour is not handled, and so are willing to follow the leader's suggestion that there is sense behind the material. The person themselves might be frightened by their disturbance: using it positively by exploring its meaning with the group may be one way of containing fear. A number of helpful interventions with this phenomenon and many others in groupwork, for example, non-cooperation, absences, attacks on one member and so on, are detailed in Whitaker's book (1985). She gives a great deal of straightforward and useable advice for the newly-fledged and the experienced practitioner.

An example of group assertiveness training

I think that learning to say 'No' and realising that you have a right to a point of view is vital in terms of mental health. Many social problems such as child molestation, drug abuse, loneliness and feelings of personal inadequacy may stem from a lack of practice in saying what you want. For this reason, student social workers are offered an option in assertion training, not only to help them to establish their own rights, but also those of their clients. At the same time they are taught to recognise the difference between assertion, non-assertion and aggression. Unfortunately, in their practice, they may have to deal with violent incidents, which can often arise when clients and others who, unable to assert themselves appropriately, deal with feelings of frustration and powerlessness with outbursts of uncontrollable behaviour (see R. Brown *et al.*, 1986, for guidelines on the management of risk).

The assertion training programme is described here: the same course pattern could be used when you are running client groups. It involves studying the basic philosophy and theory of assertiveness; recognising assertion, compliance and aggressiveness in others and oneself (we are all assertive in some situations!); identifying personal needs and goals for assertiveness; role-playing selected areas of these; visualising incidents, alternatives for improvement and the associated feelings; practising in the actual environment and learning to evaluate for oneself behaviour in everyday interactions on a long-term basis.

Three measuring tools are used in the programme (provided by Langrish, 1981):

1. At the outset an individual questionnaire is completed which checks which activities (such as refusing requests) and which people (for example, authority figures like bosses) make you feel comfortable or not.

2. From this self-assessment picture, a hierarchy of assertive behaviour is constructed. Items are identified and listed from those which are least to those which are most anxiety provoking.

3. A daily log of assertive behaviour is kept.

As you can see, this is behavioural groupwork aimed at learning new skills. The assertion training course is negotiated around these three self-report schedules, with each person choosing their particular area for change. A series of about twelve meetings, lasting around two hours, with a group size of about ten, ensures that at least one session can be devoted to each person's individual goals and regular reviews of everyone's progress. Although skills-based, group development and process are still important phenomena: the programme, though enjoyable, is none the less stressful and feelings as well as behaviours have to be dealt with by a sensitive and supportive group leader.

The groups that I have conducted have been mixed sex, closed and have dealt with a wide range of problem areas. Nevertheless it was noticeable how many social workers listed 'expressing justifiable anger' at the top of their behaviour hierarchy. Interpersonal conflict, as we have seen, may be a necessary and unavoidable part of group development; it is certainly a regular feature of social work tasks. No one chose to work on this as a goal for improvement. However, in setting up the role play scenarios, students commonly asked to replay disagreements they had had with practice teachers

or superiors when, for example, wanting to keep open a case.
It seems that the role of student may undermine attempts to
be assertive.

The participants were taught and tried the following
specific verbal and non-verbal skills, plus exercises in paying
compliments, giving and taking help (or whatever was
appropriate to individuals reaching their chosen goals for self-
improvement).

Broken record – calm repetition, saying what you want
over and over again

Fogging – receiving criticism comfortably without becoming defensive

Free information – initiating and maintaining social interaction

Negative assertion – accepting your errors and faults
(without submissive apology)

Negative inquiry – actively prompting criticism to make
your critic less dependent on manipulative ploys

Workable compromise – whenever your self-respect is not
in question, offering a workable compromise to the other
person

Avoiding non-assertive words and phrases – such as
'Would you mind very much. . .?'

Using assertive words – particularly 'I' statements such as 'I
believe'

Non-verbal skills – such as good eye contact, standing or
sitting comfortably without fidgeting and talking in a
strong steady voice.

Additionally, a 'six-step approach', which reinforces the
possibility of success, was learned. This involves preparing
beforehand; sending the assertive message; using silence;
listening reflectively to the other's point; re-sending the
message, if necessary, and focussing on solutions (Stubbs,
1985).

All these techniques are listed and described by what is now
a bourgeoning literature on this topic. The students particularly liked the down-to-earth style of Dickson's *A Woman in
your own Right: Assertiveness and You* (1982). My immediate
feedback from the groups indicated that they felt more self-

aware but were uncertain that they had acquired new skills. However I notice that ex-members, who kept up constant practice and self-vigilance, are now more confident and less 'guilty' about establishing what they want from other people. I know that their clients too will benefit by this.

To conclude I want to emphasise the need to record group sessions since this can be one of the conditions for effective work. A. Brown (1986) includes a useful section on this, so suffice it to say that the record could include the following:

Date and session number
Members and leaders present/absent
Plan for the session, for example, content and aims
Diagram of seating arrangements
Functioning of people in the session, such as participation, conflict
Individual functioning, for example, level of trust, listening
Leader's functioning, for example, what went well and what did not
Conclusion, for example, linking events to future plans and aims

To me, the most skilful groupworker will be the one who can see and record *content* – what the group talks about, and *process* – how the group handles its verbal and non-verbal transactions. One way in which I try to do this is to keep asking myself, 'What is going on here? What is the issue all about?' Noting these feelings as well as the facts promotes effective interventions.

10

Community Empowerment and Networking

It is salutary to remember that Social Services do not have a monopoly on caring. Relatives, friends and neighbours do most of the work and we are the 'junior partners' in terms of provision (Bayley, 1982). There has been a great deal of interest, therefore, in developing collaboration between these 'natural' helping networks and the formal services.

This chapter will explore the current strategies and themes in using informal, or what might better be termed 'unofficial' care. Because it is the final chapter, it also looks forward to the future of social work practice. If we are to work with a community orientation, that is, recognising and working alongside the many systems which impinge on people's lives, we may have to evolve new practice approaches. I will look back at the skills and techniques from the earlier chapters and examine which can be transferred to this type of community social work. Then I will suggest where there is a need for new skills and approaches when dealing with informal systems and caring networks.

Currently there are five main strategies for community social work: these are mutual aid networks, volunteer linking, community and client empowerment, neighbourhood help and personal networking (Froland *et al.*, 1981). I will look at all of these but will analyse the latter in some detail: personal networking is the only strategy where clear practice methods have been developed; through the use of case material, three of these methods will be illustrated – network therapy, problem-solving network meetings and network construction.

111

While patchworking, mutual aid groups, client empowerment and personal networking are all separate approaches
(although a critique of empowerment would question if it is a
value, a goal or a method), their overriding aims are the
same: they try to humanise social service bureaucracies and
make them into systems of opportunity rather than dependency; they offer scope for the recruitment and education of
local helpers who provide preventive services, community
care and self-help initiatives and they aim to give users choice
and power over service delivery and resources. (A further
aim might be to integrate housing, health, education and
other aspects of life, such as leisure.)

Using unofficial care: current strategies and themes

The health-protective effects of a strong and active network
have been known for a long time, particularly in the field of
community mental health (Caplan, 1974; Gottlieb, 1981).
Self-help groups, volunteers, neighbourhood contacts,
friends and family ties are known to lessen the effects of
unemployment and lower the incidence of depression,
domestic violence and even death (Garbarino, 1986). A
person's social circle can be an influential milieu, helping with
money, transport, job finding, child care, illness, recreation
and emotional support.

People are much more likely to seek help from informal
sources before they go to 'the welfare' (Mayer and Timms,
1970). As a result, referrals to formal agencies may stem, not
from the worsening of a problem, but from a breakdown in
informal support systems (Pottle, 1984). For example, one of
my clients was referred for residential care because her new
next door neighbour was unsympathetic to her knocking on
the wall for help; this alarm signal had worked well with the
previous tenant.

In order to take account of important care networks and to
strengthen community potential, some agencies have decen-
tralised their services to local neighbourhoods. These are
commonly known as 'patch-based systems' and research
indicates that they offer earlier interventions which are more

flexible, visible and accessible (Hadley and McGrath, 1980; Bayley *et al.*, 1984).

When the Barclay Committee examined the roles and tasks of social workers in 1982 (*'Social Workers: their Roles and Tasks'*) they paid a lot of attention to the growth of these locally-based services in trying to decide what social workers should be doing in the future. Between 1970 and 1980, Personal Social Services had become the sixth system of welfare in Britain alongside Social Security (income maintenance), Health, Housing, Education and Employment Services. Social work departments had become large, hierarchical and more widely available to a cross-section of the population. There had been growing criticism from the media, consumers and other professionals about the quality of services and whether or not they gave value for money. In general it was felt that the new generic departments were not living up to the high expectations which many people had of them.

Some demonstration projects had been set up as alternative forms of service delivery and as they were based on small geographical areas they were said to be doing 'patch work'. They were, in fact, trying to give social work a genuine base in the community by 'outposting' workers to a locality to support local carers, encourage local initiatives, develop links with other agencies at a grass roots level and break down the barriers which had arisen between professionals and citizens. They ideally served a population of about 10 000. Usually a case manager, a team of generic and specialist social workers, home helps, volunteers and neighbourhood wardens worked together, reducing bureaucracy to a minimum.

The Barclay investigation found these projects attractive, seeing that the services were more likely to be community- rather than client-centred. The workers enjoyed closer partnerships with residents, with whom they created policy. Where budgets were devolved to the neighbourhood centres, this further encouraged shared decisions about resources. Supporting informal networks, using volunteers and focusing on the context of people's lives was said by the Barclay team to aid social care planning and indirect work. If we analyse our daily tasks, we may find that the bulk of our time is actually spent on indirect work, that is, working on behalf of clients rather than in face to face contact with them. Although we communicate and negotiate with many systems, normally we do this on a case by case basis rather than engaging in social care planning on a broader front. Community social work demands a systems orientation and a change of attitude from social work about roles and tasks. Perhaps, too, new practice methods will need to evolve if we are to meet this challenge. This will be considered later.

Not unexpectedly, there were many critics of the Barclay Report's proposals about what social workers should be doing. Some of the dissenters' concerns were appended to the report. They felt that the notion of 'community' was as vague and intangible as that of 'equality': the romantic notion of 'Coronation Streets' of people who cared for as well as about one another was believed to be suspect – while friends and neighbours might be willing to look after your cat when you go on holiday, they might be less keen to help nurse a bedfast elderly person or relieve the carer of a severely disabled person.

It is known that unofficial helpers are more prepared to give assistance to someone in their neighbourhood if they live within five minutes' walking distance (Bayley, 1982). Additional criticisms centred around the fact that the experimental projects using neighbourhood models had taken place in well established solid working-class areas, not new housing estates or inner city districts. Equally the idea of using local street wardens to identify need and make direct referrals was said to undermine the social work values of respect for persons, privacy, the right to be left alone and to choose whether or not to have a service. Gossip, state intrusion, hearsay and uninvited prying into the lives of people who lived in the patch was feared by antagonists, especially if the community team began to develop links with pubs, shops and 'lollipop ladies'.

These alternative views, put to the Barclay Committee, pointed out that it was naive and optimistic to trust that we have caring networks. Social workers tend to work with people who alienate society either because they cannot cope with their lives, harm their children or are mentally ill. These 'unpopular' client groups receive less sympathy than elderly clients who have 'legitimate' incapacity and for whom the neighbourhood projects have proved most beneficial.

There remained numerous unanswered questions; for instance, about the nature of kin, friend and neighbour relations and the difference between them. Doubts were raised about the effects of engaging in partnership with local people: would this lead to a conversion of informal carers to a professional perspective, thereby eroding familiarity, intimacy and mutuality? Real partnership was thought to be a myth and upholding support networks without taking them over was thought to be an impossible balancing act: colonisation would be inevitable.

Despite these early misgivings, since 1982 more and more agencies have attempted to decentralise their structures in order to give more say to local people about their services. When managers of community social services departments were asked how 'going local' had worked, some of the advantages they mentioned were:

1. The surprise finding that, even in large cities such as London, patch-based teams had discovered unknown resources, self-help and competence amongst 'urban villages' which had traditionally been viewed as dependent and deprived.

2. The chance to adopt flexible roles among formal and informal helpers had eased innovations within departments.

3. Systems which engaged citizen participation had pushed decision making down to the grass-roots level.

4. Freer local arrangements for services had met local circumstances more appropriately.

5. Community work had become demystified; needs had become more obvious and the siege mentality of the large, hierarchical organisations was lessened.

Among the disadvantages were:

1. The reluctance of some service committees to relinquish any real power to local people in terms of resources and decision making.

2. The pointlessness of having neighbourhood centres for

field services which did not also include residential and day care facilities (equally, it would make sense to localise other community services such as housing, health, police, probation and local cash offices.)

3. Inequalities which had arisen when articulate, organised groups secured more of the budget at the expense of those even more deprived.

4. The withdrawal into the cosiness of the small locality might eventually result in a retreat from working on the major issues of poverty, oppression and unemployment.

5. The fear that unofficial care could eventually justify drastic spending cuts (see *Community Care*, 1985).

Having weighed the arguments for using informal care, volunteers, mutual aid groups and empowering communities by engaging in partnership with them, I have my own misgivings about the human costs of such programmes. We may be tacitly exploiting those who feel a moral obligation to care and, what seems to happen is that disproportionate responsibilities are managed by women in the community (Graycar, 1983).

There may be subtle pressures imposed on families to be responsible for their own problems and not to rely on state provision: increasing the burdens of carers should be resisted since this would only result in services on the cheap. Also, whilst self-help and mutual aid look fine on paper, there are occasions when such contacts are insufficient, unhelpful or even harmful. For instance, I have seen a self-help group for the parents of mentally handicapped children become 'exclusive' and offputting to new members who try to join; competition as to whose child has the 'worst' disability was another worrying feature. To prevent this, social workers could be on hand to offer consultancy and regular support to groups who are trying to manage their own difficulties. Where we see people struggling with inaccurate information, inadequate resources or attempts to exploit human kindness, we must ensure that our back-up services are guaranteed.

Despite all these concerns, plus many political ones which lie outside our scope, these initiatives towards community care, shared enterprise and recognising informal care are developing, not only in the United Kingdom but also in

America, Canada and Australia. Reports from the literature stress the successes and strains of such projects, such as the one which encouraged long-term clients, demeaned as 'problem families', to become competent, not only in running their own lives again, but in taking true citizen control over decision making and the allocation of resources in a programme set up to fight poverty (Benn, 1981). Other schemes have attempted to give clients power by setting up Family Centres whose philosophy is self-help, mutual aid, participation and openness (Fogell, 1986; Ryan, 1986). From these reports it seems that shifting from mainly formal (professional) to informal (lay) helping requires a re-examination of current practice approaches and, perhaps, the addition of new skills. This is considered before moving on to some case examples of personal networking.

Do we need new practice approaches?

Whittaker (1986) suggests that by asking social service professionals to use informal helping, we are 'charting a voyage into unfamiliar waters' (p. 41). My argument is that along the way we will encounter familiar landmarks: these will be the methods and skills outlined in earlier chapters. At the same time, dealing with social support networks and 'lay' carers requires shifts in professional attitudes and emphases plus perhaps new skills, which I shall describe below.

As far back as 1917 Mary Richmond's *'Social Diagnosis'* recorded a network intervention – it appears that there is nothing new under the sun! However in the future we shall be aiming to use a person's environment as the *instrument for change* as well as the target for it. Fortunately it has always been a tradition in social work to take into account the person-in-situation whole. This ecological perspective will be fundamental to any new approaches. The introduction of systems/unitary concepts some years ago prepared us for wide-ranging assessments but now agencies, as well as educational establishments, will need to make a commitment to integrated practice, allowing staff to work across the boundaries of individual and systems in order to gain an overarching view of what human services practice is all about.

Goals will remain the same, namely to improve social functioning and environmental change. Interpersonal and organisational abilities will be vital. An ability to get on with people will always be central and so, if you master the core therapeutic and organisational skills portrayed in earlier chapters, you will find that counselling, crisis intervention, task-centred problem solving, psychosocial understanding, behavioural therapies, working with families and groups will all be transferable to work at many levels and with one or more people.

The main difference, though, is that we have to learn to become partners as well as providers: professionals must work from a community orientation, working alongside informal carers without colonising their efforts. Similarly, as community workers have always known, there will be a need to operate on several time-scales; for instance, dealing with a crisis situation, working towards long-term preventive strategies and initiating changes which may take years to come to fruition.

Social workers can be notoriously uneasy about handling conflict (Coulshed, 1987). Workers in the public eye must be prepared for open challenges, maybe confrontations from people in the street and certainly conflicts among groups with rival loyalties and needs. Community empowerment and networking bring social workers into teams with other professionals whose knowledge and ways of working may be in marked contrast: multidisciplinary working brings its own challenges and rewards.

Working in like-minded teams is familiar territory; but the scope and reliance on mutual support and supervision is enlivened by engaging in community social work. Members of the team may include 'semi-official' people such as good neighbour groups, volunteers and paid carers who may work at a different pace, or even from opposing value positions. Skills in team-building might reduce strains in relationships and enhance corporate efforts. On the other hand working in isolation may be necessary and the practice skills involved are mentioned later when I look at the particular needs of rural social workers.

Those currently working in unstructured settings with

informal helpers report that they feel guilty about being the only paid helper; they have problems, therefore, in 'letting go' and 'taking a back seat' while others 'get on with it' (Froland *et al.*, 1981). Thus giving up total control, watching people take risks, not relying on one's 'superior' or 'expert' status, tolerating different priorities and values, coping with inevitable disruptions as helpers leave and new ones are recruited are some of the essential skills.

Teaching and consultancy may appear to be new roles and tasks but are already part of our practice wisdom. As we have seen the teaching role is part of various practice approaches (for example, behavioural): working with social supports may involve the teaching of committee skills, campaigning methods or one-to-one counselling approaches. Consultancy, too, could be viewed as a new skill, but rather it is an overlooked one: already practitioners are involved in consultancy to schools to improve the detection of child abuse; communities of interest often approach social workers to help them set up voluntary schemes when services are inadequate or non-existent. The role of network consultant has been developing over the past few years and can be seen in the growth of support groups for the relatives of physically handicapped people; a further offshoot of this has been the employment of paid carers who offer families of elderly and mentally handicapped people short- or long-term respite in their own homes, so that institutional care is avoided. The skills of employing, training and supporting carers will be basic to any community care initiatives.

There are some skills, currently viewed as specialisms, which may need to become part of everyone's domain. These include research methods, organisational analysis, social planning, financial accounting, political manoevring, media skills and managing systems. While some training courses already teach these, they will be underscored if we adopt community social work on a broader front.

There are also two specific client groups for whom we might develop new practice approaches. Firstly, people who are oppressed, such as racial minorities, could benefit from 'strategies of empowerment' which cultivate ways of overcoming that particular form of helplessness which stems from negative valuing; Solomon (1976) has begun to look at this but more work is needed in examining the dynamics and therefore the interventions which enhance practice particularly between white helpers and black clients. Secondly, rural clients, and hence rural social workers, may have to develop models of practice which take into account their special difficulties; for instance, the lack of services such as buses, shops, hospitals, schools and even social work departments (Laxton and Bennett, 1987). A social worker geographically separated from his/her team and who may also live in the 'patch', could be isolated from sources of support and supervision; it could prove difficult to draw boundaries around one's personal and public life (I sometimes had to remove compulsorily a neighbour to a mental hospital when I was a mental welfare officer); the worker as a person becomes as important as knowledge and skills.

Residents may assume that the social worker has both generalist and specialist skills and know-how and there may be an expectation that decision making will be speedy and authoritative. Sensitivity to local history and norms is essential; services have to be flexible to accommodate expressed needs and to be explained in a straightforward way – they also have to co-exist with, rather than 'cannibalise' neighbourhood efforts. Wenger (1984) found that rural dwellers were more than ready to participate in creating services which took account of local problems and possibilities.

The developments in rural social work practice could actually be used as models for community empowerment and networking in urban areas. Issues surrounding decentralisation, promoting self-help initiatives, transmitting information via the media, establishing educational groups and integrating services to improve the quality of life have already been dealt with in some Third World programmes (United Nations, 1979). Perhaps we could learn from them?

Examples of personal networking methods

It is necessary that I define the term 'personal networking', especially as networking has become a popular concept with many disciplines. I will analyse three separate strategies.

1. *Network therapy* This is a therapeutic approach where network assemblies, using large groupwork techniques, help families in crisis by bringing together their network to act as change agents (see Speck, 1967; Attneave, 1976; Rueveni, 1979). The first example is of a network assembly.

2. *Problem-solving network meetings* These bring together families and their formal carers in order to unravel non-complementary professional networks and sort out who is doing what (see Dimmock and Dungworth, 1985).

3. *Network construction* This method aims to sustain, change and build new networks. Although used originally to help chronic schizophrenic patients whose networks had become emotionally drained, toxic to them or lost through institutionalisation, it is now used to help elderly and mentally handicapped people to continue living independently in the community. Examples of this are documented by Challis and Davies' (1985) project to keep frail elderly people in their own homes, Grant's (1986) project with mentally handicapped adults and Atkinson's (1986) engagement of 'competent others' in support networks.

A network assembly

Bringing together a 'tribal' gathering to act as change agent for a family member in crisis was devised by Speck (1967). He saw that nowadays people are often lonely, keep problems to themselves or receive help from large, impersonal organisations. He invited members of a client's household, active and passive relatives, friends, neighbours, contacts from work, leisure, welfare, church and those who *knew of* the client to one or two 'healing ceremonies'. These full scale assemblies, of sometimes up to fifty people, have recently been simplified by using less participants, in partial network assemblies (Van Der Velden *et al.*, 1984).

The referral is taken by a team of three or four social workers who know and respect each other's work. A preliminary assessment interview with significant members ensures that an assembly is appropriate and that everyone understands the procedure. The family is asked to contact about a dozen members of their network and invite them to their home. The aims are to explore potential psychological and practical support and to improve communication and compassion. The skilled team aim to exploit the 'network effect', which is the result of simply bringing these people together.

The balance of the group is important. Each core member needs to have one ally, someone as a support to prevent anyone being used as a scapegoat. Representatives from the close and distant zones around the client's world allow peripheral people, who have no axe to grind to provide different perspectives, solutions and possibly more energy for emotional and task support.

The stages of helping move from convening the network to connecting members with one another ('retribalisation') and shifting responsibility for solutions from the team to the natural group. Usually, an 'ice-breaking' or introductions exercise is used to help people to relax. One social worker acts as conductor while the rest act as group facilitators. Everyone listens to each central person's view of the problem. Lists of complaints are reworded to form goals for change. Then the outsiders are asked for their solutions. Normally, polarised opinions and ideas emerge and the team use this energy to mobilise people towards change. Activists in the group push the meeting from depression to breakthrough when solutions and offers of support are given. At this point of 'exhaustion/elation' the professional team leave.

Ballard and Rosser (1979) helped a family who were subject to violent attacks from their daughter Christine, aged eighteen. Following her discharge from a psychiatric hospital they met thirty-five members of the family's network: this was really a full-scale assembly needing the space of the local vicarage. Christine's network varied in their reactions to her 'crazy' behaviour, but after venting anger they became depressed that they had not helped more. Problem solving in small groups produced offers of help with accommodation, transport, employment and renewed contact with the family. At a follow-up meeting, no tangible support had been given but the family were happy that their support network had been reformed. This had helped them to cope with Christine's outbursts without having to call in the police or social services.

A problem-solving network meeting

This is a straightforward negotiation session, developed by Garrison and Howe (1976), used by professional networks who, in helping a family, have become stuck and who need to clarify their respective roles and responsibilities. The meeting is a structured one, where everyone in turn might be asked, 'What is the problem?'; 'What have been the solutions tried so far?'; 'How can agency personnel help?' and 'What goal can everyone agree to work towards?' The purpose of the meeting and the timetable are clearly stated, then the participants are interviewed in a predetermined way which reflects the hierarchy of relationships (viz. starting with the client and the immediate support system). Everyone needs to state their position and plan; then specific tasks are delegated. Usually a follow-up meeting is needed (about three weeks later) to ensure that the agreements are working.

John was a thirty-year-old mentally handicapped man living with his brother and sister-in-law. He attended the local Adult Training Centre and had been put on probation for stealing. The Training Centre manager said that this was due to John being bored and needing a more challenging environment than he could offer. The probation officer therefore arranged for the client to attend a Life Skills course at the local college. John refused to go and his family insisted that he return to the Adult Training Centre.

When the client, family, centre manager, probation officer and social worker met under the chairmanship of the team leader, who was independent of the case, it became clear that all the agencies were working on what they thought was good for John. He and his family were very happy with the Adult Training Centre and did not want to lose contact with their friends there. Therefore he returned to this environment, with everyone's agreement.

A network construction

This involves the social worker coaching someone who wishes to sustain, build or change their network. Firstly, the person is helped to draw a network or ecomap. This is a sheet with many circles, which might represent the household, neighbours, general practitioner, school, pub, shops, club, work and so on. This is filled in using the same colour to connect who knows whom. Relationships between the client and others which are strong, weak, or stressful are depicted by different symbols, as shown in Figure 10.1. Secondly, the person is helped to assess from this the sources of interference and intimacy and, if appropriate helped to lessen or strengthen these bonds. Thirdly, overlooked sources of help are examined and the client and worker plan how these could be developed: thus, existing self-help groups might become a new part of the network; alternatively, support systems may need to be established. These may form the transitional networks from which people might begin to make their own informal ties.

Mrs Young was a thirty-five-year-old woman with one son, Paul aged twelve years. She had recently divorced her husband, who had access to his son at the weekends. Mrs Young had come to this country from Germany fifteen years previously and although living on a busy council estate knew very few people. She applied to become a foster parent to an older child. The worker helped Mrs Young to map her network to see what sources of support she would have. See Figure 10.1. As you can see from looking at the network map (and perhaps comparing it to your own), Mrs Young had a small and not very active network. Some members had strong ties with one another but the client agreed that she was very isolated and had wanted a companion for Paul. She had stopped writing to her own family in Germany. The worker encouraged her to rebuild these ties, which she did. (She is now looking forward to a holiday visit from them.) Paul's school taught German in the evenings. Mrs Young agreed to ask if they wanted any help with this. She now helps to teach German in a night-school class. She withdrew her application to foster.

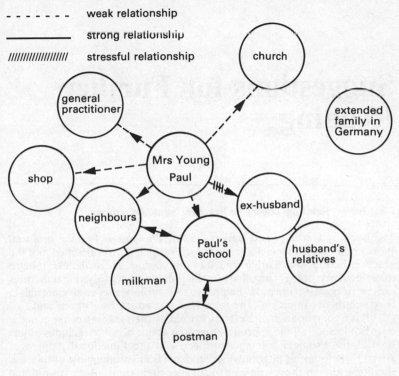

- - - - - - - weak relationship

—————— strong relationship

////////////////// stressful relationship

church

general practitioner

extended family in Germany

Mrs Young
Paul

shop

ex-husband

neighbours

Paul's school

husband's relatives

milkman

postman

Figure 10.1 *Network map*

I think that network strategies can offer exciting solutions to problems, provide more 'people muscle', reunite families with forgotten networks and give everyone the chance to offer a helping hand. Informal sources of support may yet counteract the trend towards large-scale, impersonal social services.

This book has, it is hoped, introduced some ideas by which you might improve practice competence. It is only a beginning because often a want of knowledge comes from years of study. The more I know, the more I see that I do not know. Learning from social work never ends and every client or situation teaches us this. And yet, if we show enthusiasm, admit our limitations and keep a sense of humour, this will let other people see that we are more human than otherwise.

Suggestions for Further Reading

Chapter 1   Relating Theory to Practice: Some Dilemmas

The book by Hardiker and Barker (1981), *Theories of Practice in Social Work*, relates to the social science theories which inform practice, not the practice theories which are included in this volume. Nevertheless, it helps to see how psychology, sociology, social policy and organisational theories can be applied to practice: helpfully, the authors use case material to illustrate theory-in-action. The American text edited by Roberts and Nee (1970) is a compendium of methods written by their leading proponents; it does not include all the approaches written about here but includes others such as the Problem Solving Approach and the Functional Approach. Apart from its use of jargon, which students find unintelligible at times, it should be read by those who wish to advance their knowledge of traditional theories of social casework.

Chapter 2   Assessment: the Skills of Collecting, Analysing and Understanding Information

The need for a sound assessment, on which intervention is based, is essential as the panels of inquiry into child abuse constantly show. It is worthwile looking at the criticisms contained in the Beckford Report, *A Child in Trust* (1985), and remembering that our assessments are ongoing and need to inform long-term as well as short-term work. Siporin's (1975) chapter on assessment is very thorough, while his appendix offers guidelines on how to undertake a social study. The text by Curnock and Hardiker (1979) is helpful as is that by Glampson *et al.* (1975) which addresses itself to the assessment of community needs and resources. Devore and Schlesinger (1981) give an outline of the assessment of ethnic minority communities. How to use other techniques in reaching assessments through the use of questionnaires, surveys, self perception tests, rating scales, problem checklists, sentence completion and role play exercises are illustrated by Priestley *et al.* (1978).

126

Chapter 3 Counselling and Other Ways of Influencing for Change

There are numerous books available on counselling but that by Nelson-Jones (1983) suggests exercises which can be done alone, with another person or group of people, so that readers can test their skills development: he also includes a chapter on group counselling and life skills training. You may find the books by Bandler and Grinder (1975) and Laborde (1983) rather strange at first: they deal with what seems to be a growing field – that of Neuro-Linguistic Progamming (NLP): they consider some of the techniques which can be acquired for negotiation and influencing others. However, Fisher and Ury's *Getting to Yes* is probably the best book for teaching the skills of negotiation.

Chapter 4 Crisis Intervention

The book to start with is that edited by Parad (1965; see Parad and Caplan, 1965), particularly the first two chapters which explain the theoretical frameworks of the model. The accompanying notions of loss and change, as they relate to whole societies, for example immigrants who have lost their homeland, is dealt with by Marris (1974). O'Hagan (1986) critically examines earlier texts on crisis intervention: he also considers some of the personal qualities needed by social workers when they are put under pressure to 'do something'.

Chapter 5 Task-Centred Work

All the books and articles quoted which were written by Matilda Goldberg and her colleagues demonstrate the ideas of task centred work: by consulting the bibliography in her 1985 book, *Problems, Tasks and Outcomes: the Evaluation of Task-Centred Casework in Three Settings*, the reader will be able to trace the development of this approach over the past twenty years. Most of the references contained therein, convey the relevance of research for promoting the use of practice methods.

Chapter 6 The Psychosocial Approach

For anyone seriously interested in correctly applying and understanding the concepts on which the psychosocial approach is based, it will be necessary to study the book by Hollis (1964) and to master Yelloly's (1980) text. Turner (1978) has edited several useful volumes which use case examples. Malan's (1982) fascinating book also uses patients' stories to superbly explain dynamic psychotherapy.

Chapter 7 Behavioural Social Work

The main authors to follow in the United Kingdom at the moment are Hudson (1975, 1982, 1986) and Sheldon (1984): they have written many useful articles, mainly in the *British Journal of Social Work* which demonstrate the relevance of this body of knowledge to our work with those who are mentally disordered and with children's behaviour problems. One of the chapters in the work by A. Bentovim *et al.* (see Crowe, 1982) is especially helpful for those working with couples in conflict and with sexual problems; it proposes many techniques based on learning theory.

Chapter 8   Family Work

A good introduction to what is beginning to be a highly technical field of family therapy is provided by Gorell Barnes (1984). Those who wish to advance their knowledge of some of the various models can follow the articles from the *Journal of Family Therapy*. I am particularly drawn to Haley (1976) since it is helpful for beginners who wish to feel competent in conducting interviews with more than one person. At the time of writing, we still await texts which offer more detail of ways of working with families in gender and ethnic-sensitive ways. This, though, is true of all the other social work methods.

Chapter 9   Working with Groups

There is demand for the book by Brown (1986): it offers students a quick and easy-to-read introduction to groupwork. The books by Whitaker (1985) are for those who wish to become specialists in this method. Preston-Shoot's (1986) chapters on supervision and co-leadership are useful, while the book by Zastrow (1985) contains exercises which can be used by practitioners who have the responsibility for training others to become groupworkers.

Chapter 10   Community Empowerment and Networking

No one is very sure what the term 'Community Social Work' means and therefore we still await practice methods unique to the role of community social worker. In the meantime, it is worth exploring the Barclay Report's views in *Social Workers: their Roles and Tasks* (1982) and the supplement to the *British Journal of Social Work* (1986). The ideas of networking, working with informal systems, client empowerment and participation may enhance the roles of citizen and consumer in the future requiring workers to be even more skilled and accountable.

References

A Child in Trust: the Report of the Panel of Inquiry into the Circumstances Surrounding the Death of Jasmine Beckford (1985) Published by the London Borough of Brent.

Adair, J. (1976) *Training for Decisions: a Tutor's Manual*, London, BACIE.

Algie, J. (1986) 'Weighing Up Priorities', *Community Care*, 11 September, pp. 18–20.

Alinsky, S. D. (1972) *Rules for Radicals – a Pragmatic Primer for Realistic Radicals*, New York, Vintage.

Anderson, D. (1982) *Social Work and Mental Handicap*, London, Macmillan.

Atherton, C. (1982) 'The Task Force', *Social Work Today*, vol. 14, no. 2, pp. 8–10.

Atkinson, D. (1986) 'Engaging Competent Others: a Study of the Support Networks of People with Mental Handicap', *British Journal of Social Work*, vol. 16, Supplement pp. 83–101.

Attneave, C. L. (1976) 'Social Networks as the Unit of Intervention', in Guerin, P. J. (ed.), *Family Therapy: Theory and Practice*, New York, Gardner Press.

Axelrod, R. (1984) *The Evolution of Cooperation*, New York, Basic Books.

Bailey, R. and Brake, M. (eds) (1975) *Radical Social Work*, London, Edward Arnold.

Ball, D. and Cooper, D. (1987) *Social Work and Child Abuse*, London, Macmillan.

Ballard, R. and Rosser, P. (1979) 'Social Network Assembly' in Brandon, D. and Jordan, B. (eds), *Creative Social Work*, Oxford, Basil Blackwell.

Bandler, R. and Grinder, J. (1975) *The Structure of Magic, Volume 1*, Palo Alto, Science & Behaviour Books.

Bandura, A. (1977) *Social Learning Theory*, Englewood Cliffs, N.J. Prentice-Hall.

Barclay, P. M. (1982) *Social Workers: their Roles and Tasks*, London, Bedford Square Press.

Bayley, M. (1982) 'Helping Care to Happen in the Community' in Walker, A. (ed.), *Community Care: the Family, the State and Social Policy*, Oxford, Basil Blackwell and Martin Robertson.

129

Bayley, M., Seyd, R. and Tennant, A. (1984) *Dinnington Neighbourhood Services Project: Final Report*, University of Sheffield, United Kingdom.

Beck, A. T. (1976) *Cognitive Therapy and the Emotional Disorders*, New York, New American Library.

Benn, C. (1981) *Attacking Poverty through Participation: a Community Approach*, Sydney, Pit Publishing.

Ben-Tovim, G., Gabriel, J., Law, I. and Stredder, K. (1986) *The Local Politics of Race*, London, Macmillan.

Biestek, F. P. (1965) *The Casework Relationship*, London, George Allen & Unwin.

Bowen, M. (1978) *Family Therapy in Clinical Practice*, New York, Jason Aronson.

Bowlby, J. (1982) *Attachment and Loss, Vol. 1, Attachment*, 2nd edn, London, Hogarth Press.

Box, S., Copley, B., Magagna, J. and Moustaki, E. (eds), (1981) *Psychotherapy with Families: an Analytical Approach*, London, Routledge & Kegan Paul.

Brown, A. (1984) *Consultation*, London, Heinemann Educational Books.

Brown, A. (1986) *Groupwork*, London, Heinemann Educational Books.

Brown, A. G. (1977) 'Worker Style in Social Work', *Social Work Today*, vol. 8, no. 29, 26th April, pp. 13–15.

Brown, R., Bute, S. and Ford, P. (1986) *Social Workers at Risk: the Prevention and Management of Violence*, London, Macmillan Educational.

Browne, B. (1978) *Management for Continence*, Surrey, Age Concern.

Buckle, J. (1981) *Intake Teams*, London, Tavistock Publications.

Burden, D. S. and Gottlieb, N. (1987) 'Human Behaviour in the Social Environment: the Knowledge Base for Practice', in Burden, D. S. and Gottlieb, N. (eds), *The Woman Client: Providing Human Services in a Changing World*, London, Tavistock Publications.

Burnham, J. B. (1986) *Family Therapy: First Steps Towards a Systemic Approach*, London, Tavistock Publications.

Burton, R. L. (1982) 'Group Process Demystified', *Annual for Facilitators, Trainers and Consultants*, Palo Alto, University Associates.

Butler, A. and Kerfoot, M. (1987) *Childhood and Adolescence*, London, Macmillan.

Byng-Hall, J. and Bruggen, P. (1974) 'Family Admission Decisions as a Therapeutic Tool', *Family Process*, vol. 13, no. 4, pp. 443–59.

Byng-Hall, J. and Campbell, D. (1981) 'Resolving Conflicts in Family Distance Regulation: an Integrative Approach', Journal of Marital and Family Therapy, vol. 7, no. 3, pp. 321–30.

Cade, B. W. (1982) 'Humour and Creativity', *Journal of Family Therapy*, vol. 4, no. 1, pp. 35–42.

Caplan, G. (1964) *Principles of Preventive Psychiatry*, London, Tavistock Publications.

Caplan, G. (1974) *Support Systems and Community Mental Health*, New York, Behavioural Publications.

Carlock, C. J. and Byrum-Gaw, B. (1982) 'Group Energy, Group Stage and Leader Interventions', *Annual for Facilitators, Trainers and Consultants*, Palo Alto, University Associates.

Case, L. P. and Lingerfelt, N. B. (1974) 'Name Calling: the Labelling Process in the Social Work Interview', *Social Service Review*, vol. 48, no. 1, pp. 75–86.

Challis, D. and Davies, B. (1985) 'Long-Term Care for the Elderly: the Community Care Scheme', *British Journal of Social Work*, vol. 15, no. 6, pp. 563–80.

Clough, R. (1982) *Residential Work*, London, Macmillan.

Community Care Special Issue on Decentralisation (1985) *Community Care*, 18 April, pp. 12–37.

Cooper, C. (1981) *Improving Skills in Interpersonal Relations*, Aldershot, Gower.

Corby, B. (1982) 'Theory and Practice in Long-Term Social Work: a Case Study of Practice with Social Service Department Clients', *British Journal of Social Work*, vol. 12, no. 6, pp. 619–38.

Corey, G., Corey, M. S., Callanan, P. J. and Russell, J. M. (1982) *Group Techniques*, California, Brooks/Cole.

Corrigan, P. and Leonard, P. (1978) *Social Work Practice Under Capitalism: a Marxist Approach*, London, Macmillan.

Coulshed, V. (1980) 'Process and Pitfalls of brief Consultation to Staff of Homes for the Elderly', *Social Work Service*, DHSS, September, pp. 23–8.

Coulshed, V. (1987) 'Teaching Groupwork Using the Class as "The Group", *Social Work Education*, vol. 6, no. 3.

Coulshed, V. and Abdullah-Zadeh, J. (1983) 'Case Examples of Family Therapy in a Social Services Department', *Social Work Today*, vol. 13, no. 35, pp. 11–15.

Coulshed, V. and Abdullah-Zadeh, J. (1985) 'The Side-Effects of Intervention', *British Journal of Social Work*, vol. 15, no. 5, pp. 479–86.

Crowe, M. (1982) 'The Treatment of Marital and Sexual Problems: a Behavioural Approach', in Bentovim, A., Gorell-Barnes, G. and Cooklin, A. (eds), *Family Therapy: Complementary Frameworks of Theory and Practice*, 2 vols, London, Academic Press.

Curnock, K. and Hardiker, P. (1979) *Towards Practice Theory: Skills and Methods in Social Assessments*, London, Routledge & Kegan Paul.

Dale, P., Davies, M., Morrison, T. and Waters, J. (1986) *Dangerous Families: Assessment and Treatment of Child Abuse*, London, Tavistock Publications.

Davies, M. (1984) 'Training: What We Think of it Now', *Social Work Today*, 24 January, pp. 12–17.

Davies, M. (1985) *The Essential Social Worker: A Guide to Positive Practice*, Aldershot, Gower.

Day, P. (1987) *Sociology in Social Work Practice*, London, Macmillan.

Devore, W. and Schlesinger, E. C. (1981) *Ethnic-Sensitive Social Work Practice*, St Louis C. V. Mosby Co.

Dickson, A. (1982) *A Woman in Your Own Right: Assertiveness and You*, London, Quartet.

Dimmock, B. and Dungworth, D. (1985) 'Beyond the Family: Using Network Meetings with Statutory Child Care Cases', *Journal of Family Therapy*, vol. 7, no. 1, pp. 45–68.

Doel, M. and Lawson, B. (1986) 'Open Records: the Client's Right to Partnership', *British Journal of Social Work*, vol. 16, no. 4, pp. 407–30.

Dryden, W. (ed.) (1984) *Individual Therapy in Britain*, New York, Harper and Row.

Egan, G. (1977) *Exercises in Helping Skills*, California, Brooks/Cole.

Egan, G. (1981) *The Skilled Helper: a Model for Systematic Helping and Interpersonal Relating*, California, Brooks/Cole.

Erikson, E. (1965) *Childhood and Society*, Hammondsworth, Penguin.

Evans, R. (1976) 'Some Implications of an Integrated Model for Social Work Theory and Practice', *British Journal of Social Work*, vol. 6, no. 2, pp. 177–220.

Feldman, M. P. (1966) 'Aversion Therapy for Sexual Deviations: a Critical Review', *Psychological Bulletin*, vol. 65, pp. 65–79.

Finkelhor, D. (1984) *Child Sexual Abuse: New Theory and Research*, New York, The Free Press.

Finnister, G. (1986) *Welfare Rights Work in Social Services*, London, Macmillan.

Fischer, J. (1976) *The Effectiveness of Social Casework*, New York, Charles C. Thomas.

Fisher, R. and Ury, W. (1983) *Getting to Yes*, New York, Penguin.

Fogell, C. (1986) 'Dilemmas for Staff Working in Informal Settings', *British Journal of Social Work*, vol. 16, Supplement, pp. 103–9.

Ford, K. and Jones, A. (1987) *Student Supervision in Social Work*, London, Macmillan.

Forder, A. (1976) 'Social Work and System Theory', *British Journal of Social Work*, vol. 6, no. 1, pp. 23–42.

Freire, P. (1972) *Pedagogy of the Oppressed*, Hammondsworth, Penguin Books.

Froland, C., Pancoast, D., Chapman, N. J. and Kimboko, P. J. (1981) *Helping Networks and Human Services*, Beverly Hills and London, Sage Publications.

Fromm, E. (1962) *Beyond the Chains of Illusion: My Encounter with Marx and Freud*, New York, Simon & Schuster.

Galper, J. (1980) *Social Work: a Radical Perspective*, Englewood Cliffs, N.J., Prentice-Hall.

Gammack, G. (1982) 'Social Work as Uncommon Sense', *British Journal of Social Work*, vol. 12, no. 1, pp. 3–22.

Garbarino, J. (1986) 'Where Does Social Support Fit Into Optimising Human Development and Preventing Dysfunction?', *British Journal of Social Work*, vol. 16, Supplement, pp. 23–37.

Garrett, A. (1958) 'Modern Casework: the Contributions of Ego Psychology', in Parad, H. J. (ed.), *Ego Psychology and Dynamic Casework*, New York, Family Service Association of America.

Garrison, J. E. and Howe, J. (1976) 'Community Intervention with the Elderly: a Social Network Approach', *Journal of the American Geriatric*

Society, vol. 24, pp. 329–33.

Garvin, C. D. (1981) *Contemporary Groupwork* Englewood Cliffs, NJ, Prentice-Hall.

Germain, C. (1970) 'Casework and Science: a Historical Encounter', in Roberts, R. W. and Nee, R. H. (eds), *Theories of Social Casework*, University of Chicago Press.

Gibbons, J. S., Bow, I., Butler, J. and Powell, J. (1979) 'Clients' reactions to task-centred casework: a follow-up study', *British Journal of Social Work*, vol. 9, no. 2, pp. 203–215.

Glampson, A., Scott, T. and Thomas, D. N. (1975) *A Guide to the Assessment of Community Needs and Resources*, London, National Institute for Social Work.

Glaser, D. and Frosh, S. (1987) *Child Sexual Abuse*, London, Macmillan.

Glasser, W. (1965) *Reality Therapy*, New York, Harper & Row.

Glastonbury, B. (1985) *Computers in Social Work*, London, Macmillan.

Golan, N. (1978) *Treatment in Crisis Situations*, New York, The Free Press.

Goldberg, E. M., Gibbons, J. and Sinclair, I. (1985) *Problems, Tasks and Outcomes: the evaluation of task-centred casework in three settings*, London, George Allen & Unwin.

Goldberg, E. M., Walker, D. and Robinson, J. (1977) 'Exploring the Task-Centred Casework Method', *Social Work Today*, vol. 9, no. 2, pp. 9–14.

Goldberg, E. M., Williams, B. T. and Mortimer, A. (1970) *Helping the Aged*, London, George Allen & Unwin.

Gorell Barnes, G. (1984) *Working with Families*, London, Macmillan Education.

Gottlieb, B. H. (ed.) (1981) *Social Networks and Social Support*, Beverley Hills and London, Sage Publications.

Gottman, J., Notarius, C., Gonso, J. and Markman, H. (1977) *A Couple's Guide to Communication: skills teaching for couples*, New York, Research Press Co.

Grant, G. (1986) *The Structure of Care Networks in Families with Mentally Handicapped Adult Dependants*, Working Paper from the Centre for Social Policy Research and Development, University College of North Wales, Bangor, Gwynedd.

Graycar, A. (1983) 'Informal, Voluntary and Statutory Services: the complex relationship', *British Journal of Social Work*, vol. 13, no. 4, pp. 379–94.

Hadley, R. and McGrath, M. (1980) *Going Local: neighbourhood social services*, London, National Council for Voluntary Organisations.

Haley, J. (1976) *Problem-Solving Therapy*, San Francisco, Jossey-Bass.

Hanmer, J. and Statham, D. (1987) *Women and Social Work*, London Macmillan.

Hardiker, P. and Barker, F. M. (eds) (1981) *Theories of Practice in Social Work*, London, Academic Press.

Hardiker, P. and Curnock, K. (1984) 'Social Work Assessment Processes in Work with Ethnic Minorities – the Doshi Family', *British Journal of Social Work*, vol. 14, no. 1, pp. 23–48.

Hartford, M. E. (1971) *Groups in Social Work: application of small group theory and research to social work practice*, Columbia University Press.

Henderson, P. and Thomas, D. N. (1980) *Skills in Neighbourhood Work*, London, George Allen & Unwin.

Henry, S. (1981) *Group Skills in Social Work: a four-dimensional approach*, Itasca, Illinois, Peacock.

Herbert, M. (1985) *Caring for your Children: a Practical Guide*, Oxford, Basil Blackwell.

Hollis, F. (1964) *Casework: a Psychosocial Therapy*, New York, Random House.

Hollis, F. (1970) 'The Psychosocial Approach to the Practice of Casework', in Roberts, R. W. and Nee, R. H. (eds), *Theories of Social Casework*, University of Chicago Press.

Holmes, T. H. and Rahe, R. H. (1967) 'The Social Readjustment Rating Scale', *Journal of Psychosomatic Research*, Vol. 11, pp. 213–18.

Hudson, B. L. (1975) 'An Inadequate Personality', *Social Work Today*, vol. 6, no. 16, pp. 506–8.

Hudson, B. L. (1982) *Social Work with Psychiatric Patients*, London, Macmillan.

Hudson, B. L. and Macdonald, G. M. (1986) *Behavioural Social Work: an Introduction*, London, Macmillan Education.

Hugman, B. (1977) *Act Natural*, London, Bedford Square Press.

Hutten, J. M. (1975) 'Short-Term Contracts, III', *Social Work Today*, vol. 6, no. 17, pp. 538–41.

Hutten, J. M. (1976) 'Short-Term Contracts, IV', *Social Work Today*, vol. 6, no. 20, pp. 614–19.

Industrial Society (1981) *Negotiating Skills*, Peter Runge House, 3 Carlton House Terrace, London SW1Y 5DG.

Irvine, E. E. (1966) 'Transference and Reality in the Casework Relationship', in Younghusband, E. (ed.), *New Developments in Casework: Readings in Social Work*, London, George Allen & Unwin.

Jacobs, M. (1985) *Swift to Hear: Facilitating Skills in listening and responding*, London, SPCK.

Jacobs, M. (1986) *The Presenting Past: an introduction to practical, psychodynamic counselling*, New York, Harper & Row.

James, A. L. and Wilson, K. (1986) *Couples, Conflict and Change*, London Tavistock Publications.

Jeffs, T. and Smith, M. (eds) (1987) *Youth Work*, London, Macmillan.

Jehu, D. (1975) *Learning Theory and Social Work*, London, Routledge & Kegan Paul.

Jones, D. (ed.) (1986) *Child Abuse*, London, Macmillan.

Jordan, B. (1974) *Poor Parents*, London, Routledge & Kegan Paul.

Jordan, B. (1984) *Invitation to Social Work*, Oxford, Basil Blackwell.

Jordan, B. (1987) 'Fallen Idol', *Community Care*, 12 February, pp. 24–5.

Kaufman, P. (1966) 'Helping People who Cannot Manage their Lives', *Children*, vol. 13, no. 3.

Kell, B. L. and Mueller, W. J. (1966) *Impact and Change: a Study of Counselling Relationships*, New York, Meredith Publishing Co.

Laborde, G. Z. (1983) *Influencing with Integrity*, Palo Alto, Syntony Publishing.

Langan, M. (1985) 'The Unitary Approach: a Feminist Critique', in Brook, F. and Davis, A. (eds), *Women, the Family and Social Work*, London, Tavistock Publications.

Langrish, S. V. (1981) 'Assertiveness Training', in Cooper, C. (ed.), *Improving Skills in Interpersonal Relations*, Aldershot, Gower.

Lask, J. and Lask, B. (1981) *Child Psychiatry and Social Work*, London, Tavistock Publications.

Laxton, M. and Bennett, B. (1987) 'Practice Issues in Rural Social Work', unpublished Paper, Social Work Services Group, Scotland.

Levinson, H. M. (1973) 'Use and Misuse of Groups', *Social Work*, vol. 18, no. 1, pp. 66–73.

Lindemann, E. (1965) 'Symptomatology and Management of Acute Grief', in Parad, H. J. (ed.), *Crisis Intervention: Selected Readings*, New York, Family Service Association of America.

McCaughan, N. (1977) 'Social Groupwork in the United Kingdom', in Specht, H. and Vickery, A. (eds), *Integrating Social Work Methods*, London, George Allen & Unwin.

McNeill, P. (1985) *Research Methods*, London, Tavistock Publications.

Mainprice, J. (1974) *Marital Interaction and some Illnesses in Children*, Institute of Marital Studies, The Tavistock Institute of Human Relations, London.

Malan, D. H. (1982 edition) *Individual Psychotherapy and the Science of Pychodynamics*, London, Butterworth.

Maluccio, A. N., Fein, E. and Olmstead, K. A. (1986) *Permanency Planning for Children: concepts and methods*, London, Tavistock Publications.

Marks, I. M. Boulougouris, J. and Marset, P. (1971) 'Flooding versus Desensitisation in the Treatment of Phobic Patients: a cross-over study', *British Journal of Psychiatry*, vol. 119. pp. 353–75.

Marris, P. (1974) *Loss and Change*, London, Routledge & Kegan Paul.

Marshall, M. (1983) *Social Work with Old People*, London, Macmillan.

Masters, P. (1982) 'The mentally infirm and their carers: relative's support group in Bristol', in Glendenning, F. (ed.), *Care in the Community: Recent Research and Current Projects*, Beth Johnson Foundation, Stoke-on-Trent.

Mattinson, J. (1975) *The Reflection Process in Casework Supervision*, Institute of Marital Studies. The Tavistock Institute of Human Relations, London.

Mattinson, J. and Sinclair I. A. C. (1979) *Mate and Stalemate: Working with Marital Problems in a Social Services Department*, Oxford, Basil Blackwell.

Mayer, J. E. and Timms, N. (1970) *The Client Speaks: Working-Class Impressions of Casework*, London, Routledge & Kegan Paul.

Meichenbaum, D. (1978) *Cognitive Behaviour Modification: an Integrative Approach*, New York, Plenum Press.

Minuchin, S. (1974) *Families and Family Therapy*, London, Tavistock Publications.

Minuchin, S. and Fishman, C. (1981) *Family Therapy Techniques*, Harvard University Press.

Mitchell, J. (1984) *Women: the Longest Revolution: Essays in Feminism, Literature and Psychoanalysis*, London, Virago.

Mussen, P. H., Conger, J. J. and Kagan, J. (1969) *Child Development and Personality*, New York, Harper & Row.

Nelson-Jones, R. (1983) *Practical Counselling Skills*, New York, Holt, Rinehart & Winston.

Nicolson, P. and Bayne, R. (1984) *Applied Psychology for Social Workers*, London, Macmillan.

Noonan, E. (1983) *Counselling Young People*, London, Methuen.

Northen, H. (1969) *Social Work with Groups*, Columbia University Press.

O'Hagan, K. (1986) *Crisis Intervention in Social Services*, London, Macmillan.

Oliver, M. (1983) *Social Work with Disabled People*, London, Macmillan.

Olsen, M. R. (1986); 'Integrating Formal and Informal Social Care: the Utilisation of Social Suport Networks', *British Journal of Social Work*, vol. 16, Supplement, pp. 15–22.

Open University (1982) *Parents and Teenagers*, New York, Harper & Row.

Palazzoli, M. S., Boscolo, L., Cecchin, G. and Prata, G. (1980) 'Hypothessising – Circularity – Neutrality: Three Guidelines for the Conductor of the Session', *Family Process*, vol. 19, no. 1, pp. 3–12.

Papell, C. P. and Rothman, B. (1966) 'Social Groupwork Models: Possession and Heritage', *Journal of Education for Social Work*, vol. 2, no. 2, pp. 66–77.

Parad, H. J. and Caplan, G. (1965) 'A Framework for Studying Families in Crisis', in Parad, H. J. (ed.), *Crisis Intervention: Selected Readings*, New York, Family Service Association of America.

Parkes, C. M. (1986) *Bereavement: Studies of Grief in Adult Life*, London, Tavistock Publications.

Parkinson, L. (1987) *Separation, Divorce and Families*, London, Macmillan.

Parsloe, P. and Stevenson, O. (1978) *Social Service Teams: the Practitioner's View*, London, HMSO.

Parton, N. (1985) *The Politics of Child Abuse*, London, Macmillan.

Payne, M. (1982) *Working in Teams*, London, Macmillan.

Payne, M. (1986) *Social Care in the Community*, London, Macmillan.

Penn, P. (1982) 'Circular Questioning', *Family Process*, vol. 21, no. 3, pp. 267–79.

Perlman, H. H. (1957) *Social Casework: a Problem-Solving Process*, University of Chicago Press.

Pervin, L. A. (1975) *Personality: Theory, Assessment and Research*, New York, John Wiley.

Pfeiffer, J. W. and Jones, J. E. (1975) 'Co-Facilitating', in *Annual Handbook for Group Facilitators* Palo Alto, University Associates.

Pilalis, J. and Anderton, J. (1986) 'Feminism and Family Therapy: a Possible Meeting-Point', *Journal of Family Therapy*, vol. 8, no. 2, pp. 99–114.

Pincus, A. and Minahan, A. (1973) *Social Work Practice: Model and*

Method, Itasca, Illinois, Peacock.

Pincus, L. (1975) 'How to help the Bereaved', *Social Work Today*, vol. 6, no. 13, pp. 392–5.

Pottle, S. (1984) 'Developing a Network-Orientated Service for Elderly People and their Carers', in Treacher, A. and Carpenter, J. (eds), *Using Family Therapy*, Oxford, Basil Blackwell.

Preston-Shoot, M. (1986) 'Co-Leadership in Groupwork: Decision or Drift?', in Wedge, P. (ed.), *Social Work: Research into Practice*, British Association of Social Workers. Birmingham.

Preston-Shoot, M. (1987) *Effective Groupwork*, London, Macmillan.

Priestley, P., McGuire, J., Flegg, D., Hemsley, V. and Welaham, D. (1978) *Social Skills and Personal Problem Solving: a Handbook of Methods*, London, Tavistock Publications.

Prins, H. (1975) 'Working with Psychotic Clients', *Social Work Today*, vol. 6, no. 10, pp. 294–7.

Rack, P. (1982) *Race, Culture and Mental Disorder*, London, Tavistock Publications.

Randall, R. and Southgate, J. (1980) *Cooperative and Community Group Dynamics*, London, Barefoot Books.

Rapoport, L. (1970) 'Crisis Intervention as a Brief Mode of Treatment', in Roberts, R.W. and Nee, R. H. (eds), *Theories of Social Casework*, The University of Chicago Press.

Rapoport, R. N., Fogarty, M. P. and Rapoport, R. (eds) (1982) *Families in Britain*, London, Routledge & Kegan Paul.

Redl, F. (1951) 'Art of Group Composition', in Schultze, S. (ed.), *Creative Living in a Children's Institution*, New York, Association Press.

Reid, W. J. (1967) 'A Study of Caseworkers' Use of Insight-Oriented Techniques', *Social Casework*, January pp. 3–9.

Reid, W. J. (1978) *The Task-Centred System*, Columbia University Press.

Reid, W. J. and Epstein, L. (eds) (1977) *Task-Centred Practice*, Columbia University Press.

Reid, W. J. and Epstein, L. (1972) *Task-Centred Casework*, Columbia University Press.

Reid, W. J. and Hanrahan, P. (1981) 'The Effectiveness of Social Work: recent evidence', in Goldberg, E. M. and Connolly, N. (eds), *Evaluative Research in Social Care*, London, Heinemann.

Reid, W. J. and Shyne, A. W. (1969) *Brief and Extended Casework*, Columbia University Press.

Richmond, M. E. (1917) *Social Diagnosis*, New York, Russell Sage.

Richmond, M. E. (1922) *What is Social Case Work?*, New York, Russell Sage.

Roberts, R. W. and Nee, R. H. (eds) (1970) *Theories of Social Casework*, University of Chicago Press.

Rogers, C. (1980) *A Way of Being*, Boston, Mass., Houghton Mifflin.

Rueveni, U. (1979) *Networking Families in Crisis*, New York, Human Sciences Press.

Ryan, P. J. (1986) 'The Contribution of Formal and Informal Systems of Intervention to the Alleviation of Depression in Young Mothers', *British*

Journal of Social Work, vol. 16, Supplement, pp. 71–82.

Sainsbury, E. (1986) 'The Contribution of Client Studies to Social Work Practice', in Wedge, P. (ed.) *Social Work – Research into Practice*, British Association of Social Workers. Birmingham.

Saunders, D. G. (1984) 'Helping Husbands who Batter', *Social Casework*, vol. 65, no. 6, pp. 347–53.

Scherz, F.H. (1970) 'Theory and Practice of Family Therapy', in Roberts. R. W. and Nee, R. H. (eds), *Theories of Social Casework*, University of Chicago Press.

Schless, A. P., Teichman, A., Mendels, J. and Di Giacomo, J. N. (1977) 'The Role of Stress as a Precipitating Factor of Psychiatric Illness', *British Journal of Psychiatry*, vol. 130, pp. 19–22.

Scott, D. and Starr, I. (1981) 'A twenty-four-hour family-orientated psychiatric crisis service', *Journal of Family Therapy*, vol. 3, no. 2, pp. 177–86.

Scott, M. (1983) *Group Parent-Training Programme*, Liverpool Personal Service Society, Stanley Street, Liverpool L1 6AN.

Scott, M. and Ross, M. (1986) *An Evaluation of Individual and Group Cognitive Therapy in the Treatment of Depression*, Liverpool Personal Service Society.

Seligman, M. E. P. (1975) *Helplessness: On Depression, Development and Death*, San Fransisco, Freeman.

Shaffer, J. B. P. and Galinsky, M. D. (eds), (1974) *Models of Group Therapy and Sensitivity Training*, Englewood Cliffs, N. J. Prentice-Hall.

Sheldon, B. (1983) 'The Use of Single-Case Experimental Designs in the Evaluation of Social Work', *British Journal of Social Work*, vol. 13, no. 5, pp. 477–500.

Sheldon, B. (1984) 'Behavioural Approaches with Psychiatric Patients', in Olsen, M. R. (ed.), *Social Work and Mental Health*, London, Tavistock Publications.

Shulman, L. (1979) *The Skills of Helping: individuals and groups*, Itasca, Illinois, Peacock.

Siporin, M. (1975) *Introduction to Social Work Practice*, London, Collier Macmillan.

Smid, G. and van Krieken, R. (1984) 'Notes on Theory and Practice in Social Work: a comparative view', *British Journal of Social Work*, vol. 14, no. 1, pp. 11–22.

Smith, C., Lane, M. and Walshe T. (1987) *Court Work*, London, Macmillan.

Smith, C. R. (1983) *Social Work with the Dying and Bereaved*, London, Macmillan.

Smith, L. L. (1979) 'Crisis Intervention in Practice', *Social Casework*, February, pp. 81–8.

Solomon, B. B. (1976) *Black Empowerment: social work with oppressed communities*, Columbia University Press.

Speck, R. V. (1967) 'Psychotherapy of the Social Network of a Schizophrenic Family', *Family Process*, vol. 7, pp. 208–14.

Steinhauer, P. D. (1984) 'Clinical Applications of the Process Model of Family Functioning', *Canadian Journal of Psychiatry*, vol. 29, March, pp. 98–111.

Stevenson, O. (1963) 'The Understanding Caseworker', *New Society*, 1 August, pp. 84–96.

Stubbs, D. R. (1985) *How to use Assertiveness at Work*, Aldershot Gower.

Thomas, E. J. (1970) 'Behavioural Modification and Casework' in Roberts, R. W. and Nee, R. H. (eds), *Theories of Social Casework*, University of Chicago Press.

Timms, N. (1983) *Social Work Values: an Enquiry*, London, Routledge and Kegan Paul.

Toole, S. and Winfield, M. (1986) 'Expert Systems and their Implications for Social Workers', *Computer Applications in Social Work and Allied Professions*, vol. 3, no.1, pp. 19–22.

Treacher, A. and Carpenter, J. (eds), (1984) *Using Family Therapy*, Oxford, Basil Blackwell.

Trower, P., Bryant, B. and Argyle, M. (1978) *Social Skills and Mental Health*, London, Methuen.

Tsoi, M. and Yule, J. (1982) 'Building Up New Behaviours: shaping, prompting and fading', in Yule, W. and Carr, J. (eds), *Behaviour Modification for the Mentally Handicapped* London, Croom Helm.

Tuckman, B. W. and Jensen, M. A. C. (1977) 'Stages of Small Group Development Revisited', *Group and Organisation Studies*, vol. 2, no. 4, pp. 419–27.

Tunstill, J. (1987) *Child Care*, London Macmillan.

Turner, F. J. (1978) *Psychosocial Therapy: a Social Work Perspective*, New York, The Free Press.

Twelvetrees, A. (1985) *Community Work* London, Macmillan.

United Nations (1979) *Social Services in Rural Development: issues concerning their design and delivery*, United Nations, New York.

Van Der Velden, H. E. M., Halevy-Martinin, J., Ruhf, L. and Schoenfield, P. (1984) 'Conceptual Issues in Network Therapy', *International Journal of Family Therapy*, vol. 6, no. 2, pp. 68–81.

Vickery, A. (1976) 'A Unitary Approach to Social Work with the Mentally Disordered', in Olsen, M. R. (ed.), *Differential Approaches in Social Work with the Mentally Disordered*, British Association of Social Workers. Birmingham.

Walker, H. and Beaumont, B. (eds) (1985) *Working with Offenders*, London, Macmillan.

Walrond-Skinner, S. (1976) *Family Therapy: the Treatment of Natural Systems*, London, Routledge & Kegan Paul.

Walrond-Skinner, S. (ed), (1979) *Family and Marital Psychotherapy: a Critical Approach*, London, Routledge & Kegan Paul.

Watzlawick, P. (1978) *The Language of Change: Elements of Therapeutic Communication*, New York, Basic Books.

Wenger, G. C. (1984) *The Supportive Network: Coping with Old Age*, London, George Allen & Unwin.

Whan, M. (1983) 'Tricks of the Trade: Questionable Theory and Practice in Family Therapy', *British Journal of Social Work*, vol. 13, no. 3 pp. 321–38.

Whitaker, D. S. (1975) 'Some Conditions for Effective Work with Groups', *British Journal of Social Work*, vol. 5 no. 4, p. 423–40.

Whitaker, D. S. (1985) *Using Groups to Help People*, London, Routledge & Kegan Paul.

Whittaker, J. K. (1986) 'Integrating Formal and Informal Care: a conceptual framework', *British Journal of Social Work*, vol. 16, Supplement, pp. 39–62.

Winnicott, D. W. (1957) 'The Capacity to Be Alone', paper read at a meeting of the British Psychoanalytical Society, 24 July.

Wittenberg, I. S. (1970) *Psychoanalytic Insight and Relationships: a Kleinian Approach*, London, Routledge & Kegan Paul.

Wootton, B. F. (1959) *Social Science and Social Pathology*, London, George Allen & Unwin.

Yalom, I. D. (1970) *The Theory and Practice of Group Psychotherapy*, New York, Basic Books.

Yelloly, M. A. (1980) *Social Work Theory and Psychoanalysis*, Wokingham, Van Nostrand Reinhold.

Zastrow, C. (1984) 'Understanding and Preventing Burnout', *British Journal of Social Work*, vol. 14, no. 2, pp. 141–56.

Zastrow, C. (1985) *Social Work with Groups*, Chicago, Nelson-Hall.

Index